THE
LITTLE
BOOK
OF
CARDIFF

THE
LITTLE
BOOK
OF
CARDIFF

DAVID COLLINS &
GARETH BENNETT

The
History
Press

First published 2015

The History Press
The Mill, Brimscombe Port
Stroud, Gloucestershire, GL5 2QG
www.thehistorypress.co.uk

British Library Cataloguing in Publication Data.
A catalogue record for this book is available from the British Library.

ISBN 978 0 7509 5959 9

Typesetting and origination by The History Press
Printed and bound in Great Britain by TJ International Ltd.

CONTENTS

FOREWORD

I have seen so many changes in Cardiff, so many changes in South Wales.

I came to Cardiff after the Second World War. Before the war, I was a miner in Blackwood. I come from a world of pit ponies, pennant slab floors and chitlins for dinner. But the city of Cardiff offers a hearty welcome to outsiders – if they are willing to 'make a go of it' – as well as its own. And so, in time, this boy from Blackwood made it to Lord Mayor of the capital city of Wales.

Sometimes I shake my head at the memory and ask myself, 'How did that happen?' And sometimes I look at all the changes in the city over the years and I ask myself the same question.

This book has brought back so many memories for me. Of Tiger Bay, Shirley Bassey, Cardiff City FC – where, for my sins, I was a season-ticket holder for fourteen years – and, of course, the rugby. The whole city is spread out before you in these pages.

It has also got me thinking of other things, which are not included in these pages. Of political battles for the old Cardiff Central ward. Of so many names and faces that helped to shape the city. And of schemes which were proposed, but never came into being – like the Hook Road development, which would have cut Cardiff in half. They even wanted to knock down the Animal Wall once. I wasn't having that!

In this book you can read about long-demolished steel-works, pubs that have been lost but not forgotten and the origins of our leafy suburbs. About life in Splott, Ely and Rhiwbina. About the finest civic centre in the country – and Caroline Street. It's a colourful tale of the ever-changing tapestry of our city.

But this book is not all about the past. It's about the present and even the future of the city. For, like time and the River Taff itself, our city flows ever on.

I was pleased to support this book. I hope you enjoy the many stories the boys unfold.

Here's another one, which I was proud to share with them: Many towns and cities have a mayor. Some have a Lord Mayor. But only five have a Right Honourable Lord Mayor, and Cardiff is one of them! There are few other places like Cardiff.

Enjoy the book.

Foreword by William Penry Milwarden Herbert
Rt Hon. Lord Mayor of Cardiff, 1988–89
(But you can call me Bill!)

INTRODUCTION

This is a book about Cardiff. There have been books about Cardiff before, but we have written another one.

Why have we written it? Well, we wrote a couple of books about Cardiff City Football Club and our publishers, The History Press – who have printed a series of books about different cities, entitled *The Little Book of …* – asked us if we wanted to do *The Little Book of Cardiff*. So we said yes.

We have read some of the other books about Cardiff, and about parts of Cardiff. Many of them are built around photograph collections. Photos of 'old Cardiff' are a wonderful thing, which often show vividly (and more vividly than words) how Cardiff used to be. We have used some photos to help illustrate the book, but this is not primarily a photo collection.

We have tried to put everything we could think of that was interesting about Cardiff into this book. Ultimately, we had to leave a whole load of things out, because there was a limit to how much we could fit into the space. Hopefully it will be a bit different from other books that have been published about Cardiff. And maybe, if enough readers find it interesting, we might put the rest of the stuff into *The Little Book of Cardiff, Volume II*.

The year 2015 is a fairly momentous one for Cardiff. It marks 110 years since the place was granted city status (in 1905) and sixty years since it was officially designated as the capital city of Wales (in 1955). Perhaps equally importantly, the proliferation of 'big-name' stores in the city centre, and the run of major football finals that the Millennium Stadium has staged in recent years, have put the city very much 'on the map' as a leisure and tourist destination for people throughout the UK – and further afield. Cardiff is now, for instance, a frequent location for stag and hen weekends, which has added to the colour of the city's nightlife.

A couple of other quick points: This book has been put together by two people and we have presented it in two different fonts, so that the readers can see who has written what. So Gareth's stuff is written like this, *and David's is written like this.*

This is a book about both the present and the past. I (Gareth) have been around for only a small bit (45 years) of this past, and David for a few years longer. But neither of us are 'as old as Methuselah'. We have drawn our material not only from our own experiences, but also from printed sources and from the memories of people older than us.

Mistakes can sometimes arise, however, due to ignorance, misconceptions, misunderstandings, 'urban mythology' and even – heaven forbid! – false memories. I have been the principal editor of this work, so the final responsibility for such mistakes lies with me. If you do find any then I apologise in advance. But I hope there will only be a small number. Fingers crossed ...

Gareth Bennett
2015

1

CARDIFF – WHERE'S 'AT, THEN?

An initial question: why is Cardiff there at all? I mean, why did they build a town in that exact spot? First of all, we will have to do a little bit of geography. But don't worry, it won't take long, and I'll try not to make it too boring.

THE TWISTS OF THE TAFF

First things first, then: why is Cardiff there at all?

The answer to that question lies in a little stream that forms in some mountains up in mid-Wales, called the Brecon Beacons. This burbling backwater trickles for a bit, then joins another small brook. After dribbling on a bit further, twisting this way and that, it becomes a recognisable river. It has a name, too: the *Taf Fawr* or, in English, the Big Taff. A bit further on, a tributary joins it (the *Taf Fechan*, or Little Taff) and it becomes a bigger river. It gets less waggly and begins to flow in a distinctly southerly direction.

Our river wends its way through mountain passes and then drops down, forming a narrow valley. This is the Taff Valley. Eventually the people living in the whole region of Wales bore the nickname, lent by this river, of 'Taffies'. (This tag of 'Taffy' sometimes amuses people from North Wales, who grew up living nowhere near the River Taff.)

There is nothing particularly special about the Taff. There are many other rivers like it, running south from these mighty mountains – the Beacons – into the Bristol Channel. These include the Usk, the Ogmore, the Afan, the Neath and the Tawe and their many tributaries. Together these rivers form a distinctive region known today as 'the South Wales Valleys'.

Let's forget about these other rivers now and concentrate on our river: the Taff. The River Taff, now in a narrow valley, carries on running south and is enlarged by the water running into it from its own various tributaries. The Cynon runs into it from the west, followed by the Rhondda. From the other side, a smaller river, the Taff Bargoed, joins it.

The Taff continues to work its way south, until the valley widens and almost vanishes, becoming instead a wide gorge (the Taff Gorge). Then the river enters a wide floodplain, flows for a few miles further, and empties into the sea at a large bay.

This bay was once called Tiger Bay, but is known today as Cardiff Bay. Around this bay, and in the floodplain, was built a town, and this town became known as Cardiff. In time, the town became a city. This book is about that city.

A Bit of History (Not Much, Mind)
We are going back a bit now, just for a little while, so bear with us. We are going back to the year 50 BC.

In those days, the whole of Britain was inhabited by people who spoke various Celtic dialects, all of them related to the language we now call 'Welsh'. So you have to imagine a Britain where nobody spoke any English.

There was no single ruler of the island, as there were thirty-odd different Celtic tribes, each with their own chief. So, at this time, there was no England, Scotland or Wales, there was just one island, with about thirty different 'countries' or tribal territories contained within it.

THE SILURES – THE ORIGINAL CELTIC WARRIORS

In what we now know as Wales, there were three main Celtic tribes. In south-east Wales, the area that concerns us, were the Silures.

The Silures farmed the rich pastures of the Vale of Glamorgan. The Vale is a flat area just west of Cardiff, where calcium carbonate deposits in the soil have created fertile farmland. However, before the Celts came over from south-western Europe (possibly Spain) in about 500 BC, nobody knew how to farm this area.

The problem was that lowland soils were harder to plough than upland soils. The ancient people who were in Britain before the Celts used wooden ploughs, which were not strong enough to break up this soil, so the Celts introduced iron ploughs. Soon the soil was suitable for rearing cattle (who also pulled the ploughs) and growing crops. Thus began the agricultural tradition of the Vale of Glamorgan, which continues to this day.

The Silures also fashioned tools and weapons out of bronze and iron, and made clothes. They lived in huts with roofs of arched timber and walls made of wicker and thatch. Their religion involved worshipping sun gods and their priests were called Druids. They also had some chaps who wrote poetry, who were called bards. These were important too, because there was no written language yet, so the bards related the history of the tribe through poems and folk songs, which were passed from one generation to the next.

The Silures were mainly peaceful. But then again, you would not want to mess with them – they did not make their weapons for nothing. They built a large hill fort just west of the River Ely, called Caerau. From there, Silure watchmen could look down and spy the approach of any invading tribes.

The Silure kingdom extended from, roughly, the River Wye in the east, to the River Loughor in the west. Beyond the Loughor lay the land of the Demetae, a different Celtic tribe. The Brecon Beacons formed a northern frontier, a large physical barrier between the Silures and the Ordovices of North Wales. To the south lay the Bristol Channel, and across the channel lived the Dumnonii.

Although these tribes shared similar cultures and dialects, they did not regard one another as 'fellow Celts'. That is a label that has been given to them by the professors of today, to distinguish them from other ethnic groups, such as the Anglo-Saxons, who came to Britain later. At the time in which they lived, the Silures and the other tribes were quite likely to fall out – over a border dispute, for instance, or persistent cattle-rustling – and start a war against one another.

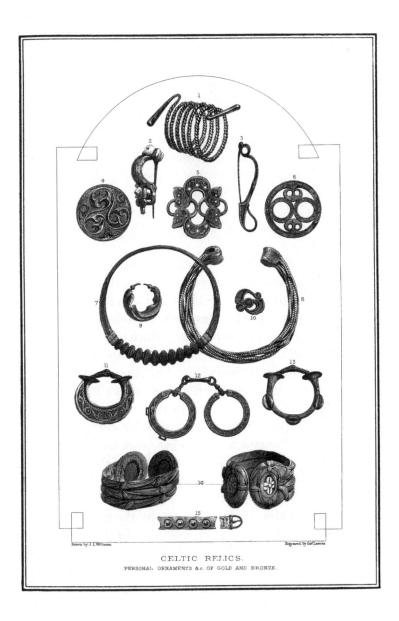

CELTIC RELICS.
PERSONAL ORNAMENTS &c. OF GOLD AND BRONZE.

When they fought, the Celtic tribes fought hard. They often raced into battle naked, covered from head to foot in blue paint called woad, screaming at the top of their voices like banshees. (Not Siouxsie and the Banshees, just banshees. If you don't know what a banshee is, Google it!) When they killed rival tribesmen, they tended to cut their heads off and hang them on their belts. Nice.

However, the Celtic tribes were not always fighting one another. In times of peace, there was trading between them. Trade also went on with other Celtic tribes who lived in France and north-western Spain.

THE ROMAN INVASION OF SOUTH WALES

The Dumnonii had discovered tin down in Cornwall and began mining it. Some of the tin was shipped over to the Continent and sold or exchanged for luxury goods like wine and pottery. The Demetae in West Wales had similarly discovered gold in the Towy Valley, which they exported.

The British trade in tin and gold came to the attention of the Romans, who were busy building a huge empire spreading out from the Mediterranean. The Roman leaders decided that, if this island, Britain, had large deposits of tin, iron ore and gold, then it might be worth 'having a look at'. The Romans didn't bother much with trade treaties and such like; they had a large army, so they normally just 'sent the boys in'. So, in AD 43, the Roman invasion of Britain began.

In South Wales, the Silures, led by the great warrior **Caradoc**, put up a fierce resistance. But the Romans had a clever idea. They thought that if they controlled the coast and the rich coastal plain of the Vale, the Silures would be forced up into the mountains, where it would be difficult for them to live. The Roman military leaders saw the River Taff

flowing into the sea at the big bay and thought this would be an excellent place to build a proper castle.

So in AD 55, the Romans constructed this castle on the banks of the Taff. They built a bridge at the first place up the river where it was feasible to do so (Canton Bridge). Then they built their fort on the east side of the bridge. The castle still stands in the same place today.

This castle also gave Cardiff its name. The Silures saw the castle, gasped in wonderment at the solid construction, and named it *Caerdaff*, meaning 'Fort on the Taff'. Over the years, the name mutated into *Caerdyf* and then *Caerdydd*. This name proved to be too tongue-twisting for the later settlers – the English – who changed it to Cardiff. To the Welsh speakers, it is still *Caerdydd*.

The Silures carried out guerrilla warfare from the mountains for a few years, but eventually had to give in and make peace on the Romans' terms.

After that, everything changed. The Romans built a series of forts to control coastal Wales. The main one was at Caerleon, where their troops were garrisoned. Modern roads were then built linking these forts. One linked Caerleon with Cardiff and Neath: the original A48! Another one went from Ystradgynlais, across the heads of the Valleys, then down the Rumney Valley to Cardiff – the last section being the original North Road.

The Celtic leaders now spoke and wrote in the Roman language of Latin and adopted Roman culture. This persisted for 350 years, until around AD 400. Then, the Roman troops had to evacuate Britain to deal with threats to Rome from northern barbarians called Goths.

Nobody is now sure how many people remained in Cardiff after the Roman soldiers left. It may be that the fort was abandoned and that there was only a very small community of subsistence farmers left in the area.

ENGLAND AND WALES

One of the main things about Cardiff is that it is the capital of Wales. It is also the largest city or town in Wales.

But why is there a 'Wales' separate from 'England' at all? This is a question that puzzles many people in England – I know, because I used to live there.

Well, once the Romans left, there was a political vacuum in Britain. The Celts were now more united than before, with one leader, known as **Vortigern**, who came to power in about AD 425. But there was still a tendency for the Celts to revert to their old tribal differences – so nobody was very sure how united Britain would be if it came under attack once again.

A significant ethnic minority during this era was the **English** (or **Angles**). These were fair-haired people from Northern Europe – from the areas we now call Holland, north-western Germany and Denmark. They began to come to Britain during the Roman occupation, as soldiers working for the Romans. Many of them, after retiring, were allowed to settle in Britain, and English communities began to spring up on the east coast.

To the north of Britain, beyond the wall which the Roman emperor Hadrian had built, lived a fierce, warlike tribe of Celts who had never accepted Roman rule. These were the Picts. Vortigern was worried that, with the Romans gone, the Picts would launch sea-borne attacks on Britain's east coast. To prevent this, he encouraged more English to settle on the coast, granting them land in return for defending the coast. This turned out to be a disastrous political policy instigated by Vortigern, as in around AD 440 the English mutinied against their Celtic rulers and tried to establish their own independent kingdom.

This began 250 years of warfare between the Celts and the English. It ended with the English living (in seven different kingdoms) in an area which eventually became known as **England**, while the Celts were pushed west into an area which became known as **Wales**.

A Note on Ethnic Terms

A quick note here on terminology: the Celts, whom we will now call the Welsh, did not call the English 'English'. Their Celtic word for them was *saes,* meaning foreigner. From *saes* we also have similar words, such as *saeson* and *saesneg*. We also get variations like *sassenach* (a Pictish, and later Scottish word for the English) and *saxon*.

Mostly, though, these foreigners called themselves *Angles*, as many were from the area of Angeln, between Germany and Denmark. Their term of *Angleland* for their new land was eventually shortened to *England*; and so the Angles became the English.

The Angles' name for foreigner, at this time, was *wylisc*. From this term we get the word Welsh – and also the Angles' name for the land of these Welsh: Wales.

Of course, the Welsh didn't call themselves 'Welsh' at this time. They called themselves and their land *Combrogi* or *Cymru*, and their language *Cymraeg*. (Other variations include *Cambria* and *Cumbria*, which remained Welsh for a long time.)

In AD 780, one of the Saxon kings, Offa of Mercia, started to build a huge earthworks (Offa's Dyke) to signify the border between 'England' (which now consisted of three Saxon kingdoms of Northumbria, Mercia and Wessex) and 'Wales'.

Hopefully that's cleared up how 'Wales' and 'England' came into being. Now we need to get back to Cardiff …

THE NORMAN TAKEOVER OF SOUTH WALES

In 1066, the situation in England was transformed by another invasion. The Normans, a bunch of French-speaking Viking descendants, sailed over and beat the Saxons (aka the English). Led by William the Conqueror, they then took over the whole of England.

This need not have affected Wales, but the Normans were a greedy bunch, who 'wanted the lot'. They quite fancied the nice farmland in the Vale of Glamorgan and, further west, in Pembrokeshire. William needed to reward the Norman lords who had sailed over with him, and whose men had fought for him. He did this by awarding them land.

As the Normans had not conquered the Welsh, Wales was at first left alone. But then William's son, King William II, awarded his mate **Robert Fitzhamon** the title of 'Baron of Gloucester'. Fitzhamon reckoned this title meant he 'owned' the whole of South Wales. He moved his forces west across the Wye in around 1090 and quickly took possession of the old

Roman fort at Cardiff, which was then rebuilt in the Norman style. From this base he set about taking over South Wales, and by the end of the century the conquest was complete.

Fitzhamon ruled everything south of the Brecon Beacons, from Gloucester to Cardigan. He was one of the so-called Marcher Lords, who built castles along the Welsh border and coastline to keep the unruly Welsh hemmed in.

For a while, Wales retained some independence. But by 1536–42, when the so-called 'Acts of Union' were passed, the region had come totally within the jurisdiction of English law and government. **John Bassett** became the first MP to represent 'Cardiff Boroughs' in the English Parliament that year.

Of course, there was still a massive cultural difference between England and Wales: the most obvious being that the common people of Wales all spoke Welsh. But in constitutional terms, it could be argued that 'Wales' after 1542 was, more or less, part of 'England'.

Yes, I know, we are getting off the subject again. When are we going to get back to Cardiff? Well, we are just getting there. Now, in a minute.

FROM THE NORMANS TO THE AGE OF THE 'BLACK GOLD'

Okay, back to the story of Cardiff. We have covered a few invasions now, and it may be getting confusing. To sum them up: the Romans built Cardiff Castle and established the town; the Saxons pushed the Welsh out of England and into Wales, but didn't get to Cardiff. The Normans *did* get to Cardiff, and took over the castle – and the town.

We have missed out the Vikings, who raided the South Wales coast in between the Saxon and Norman invasions, in around AD 850. They seem to have used Cardiff as a base during this period, and some Cardiff street names – such as Womanby Street and Dumballs Road – supposedly derive their names from Viking terms.

One imagines the Viking ships sailing up the Taff to just below Canton Bridge, which had become a dock. You have to picture Westgate Street as being the course of the river, which it was way back then, before the river was redirected to run west of it. So what is now Quay Street led from St Mary Street to an actual quay, where ships were loaded and unloaded. Further up from Canton Bridge, the river became quite twisty and unnavigable.

But the Vikings did not conquer South Wales or settle here. They came, they moored, they raped and pillaged, drank some pots of lager – and then they left.

Back to the Normans. After the Norman lords moved into Cardiff Castle, the township around the castle began to grow. Town walls were built, with gates at western and eastern ends (hence Westgate Street), and by 1126 a local Norman bigwig had become the town's first mayor.

However, having an imposing stone castle in the centre of town did not guarantee that there would not be 'disturbances' from time to time. Welsh feudal chiefs did not like their loss of power to the Normans, and every so often there would be a rebellion. In 1158, **Ifor Bach**, the Welsh lord of Senghenydd, attacked the castle and carried off the local Norman ruler, **William, Earl of Gloucester**.

There were further attacks on the castle in 1294 and 1315. Then, in 1404, the last Welsh tribal uprising occurred when **Owain Glyndwr** and his merry rebels rolled into town and seized the castle. But again, the Normans put the revolt down and Glyndwr was forced to flee. These episodes are commemorated in the names of two current town-centre drinking spots: the Clwb Ifor Bach and the Owain Glyndwr – both within spitting distance of the castle.

The Normans had created the title of 'Lord of Glamorgan', and whoever held this title had the ownership of the castle. Initially, the lordship was part of the barony (and later the earldom) of Gloucester, and some of the Lords of Glamorgan became important figures in the English court. **Hugh Despenser**, for instance, became Edward II's principal adviser, until he was overthrown by his rival Roger Mortimer. Despenser, a rather nasty man himself, then suffered an horrendous execution in London, involving hanging (although not until dead), live disembowelment and then beheading – all performed to the merriment of the huge crowd. (Doubtless, though, he would have been overjoyed to know that his name lived on to this day in Despenser Gardens, a small park in Riverside.)

In 1536, the Normans set up a new system of local government in South Wales. 'Glamorgan' now became a county based on the English (Saxon) model, with Cardiff as its county town. **William Herbert***, a fierce soldier who had become a favourite of Henry VIII, became the first Baron Cardiff (as well as Earl of Pembroke) and was, therefore, owner of the castle. Herbert's son **Henry Herbert** inherited these titles and was, in addition, made Admiral of South Wales – responsible for defending the coast – and Lord President of Wales, meaning he chaired the Council of Wales and the Marches. Cardiff was becoming a major centre of regional administration.

In 1542, the town became a 'free borough', and in 1608 it received a royal charter from King James I. In 1610, **John Speed** published the earliest-known map of the town (which he spelled 'Cardyfe'). It shows a still very small and compact town, bounded by its four gates: the West Gate, close to where the Angel Hotel now stands; the North Gate, by the junction of Kingsway and North Road; the East Gate, a small distance away; and the South Gate, which was close to the monument end of what is now St Mary Street.

In the 1640s, there was more excitement as the English Civil Wars 'kicked off'. Forces loyal to Charles I marched from Pembroke to Cardiff Castle and Oliver Cromwell's Roundheads shelled the castle from a raised spot a mile west of it. (This is where the King's Castle pub in Canton was later built.) There was a major battle at St Fagans, which the Roundheads won.

Peace returned to the Cardiff area, which from the 1770s was ruled not by the Herberts but by the Stuarts (later the Crichton-Stuarts), who married into the Herbert family. The first Stuart to own the castle was **John Stuart**, titled Lord Mount Stuart and, later, the 1st Marquess of Bute.

---

*I should add at this point that William Herbert is not the same Bill Herbert who wrote the Foreword to this book. Bill is knocking on a bit in years, it is true, but he is not that ancient!

The Butes continued to own, and sometimes to reside in, Cardiff Castle until the 1940s. By this time, though, Cardiff had been completely transformed by stuff that was dug out of the hills to the north of the town.

This stuff was known as 'black gold'. Today we just call it 'coal'.

THE TWISTS OF THE TAFF CONTINUED

In the 1800s, large deposits of precious minerals were discovered in these mountains: first iron ore and then coal. As Britain entered the Industrial Revolution, these minerals were found to be extremely useful. Iron ore was needed to make steel, a hardy material that was used for building bridges and railway lines; coal was used for powering trains and ships. As other countries looked at Britain's increasing prosperity and 'got the hang' of this industry thing, they wanted our coal, too, so it was shipped out to them.

Landowners in the hills of South Wales began to employ surveyors to search for these precious deposits. Ironworks began to sprout up, followed by coalmines.

Where the River Taff dropped down from the mountains and began to form its valley, a large town grew. It was called Merthyr Tydfil. There were ironworks there, and then coalmines. People were needed to work these enterprises, and poor farm labourers left their homes in rural Wales and trooped into Merthyr to sign up. But there were not enough farm labourers in Wales to go around, and so these men were joined by others from further afield: yokels from the West Country and, later (and controversially), Irish navvies.

Within a generation, Welsh had been displaced as the local tongue in favour of English – spoken, initially, in a variety of different dialects. A generation after that, this melting pot of accents combined to produce a new one: the accent of the Taff Valley.

Other towns were forming along the other valleys, as more mineral deposits were found. Soon, more iron-works and, especially, coalmines were started up. Up in the Cynon Valley, major settlements emerged at Aberdare and Mountain Ash; in the Rhondda, there was Maerdy, Treorchy, Porth and Tonypandy.

Where the Rhondda ran into the Taff, another biggish town developed, called Pontypridd. But so much coal was now being dug out of the ground, it was becoming hard for the packhorses to carry it along the primitive cart tracks alongside the River Taff. Some new innovation was needed.

This took the form of a canal, dug by the navvies during the 1790s, which ran alongside the Taff from Merthyr all the way to Cardiff's docks. This was the Glamorganshire Canal.

Within a few years, there was so much coal being dug out of the Valleys that the canal no longer sufficed, and a railway line was built. Soon there were passenger services, as well as freight. This line was called the Taff Vale Railway.

Where the river ran into the sea at Cardiff Bay, new and bigger docks were constructed, so that greater quantities of coal could be loaded on to the endless procession of ships. The ships sent the coal all the way around the world. By 1906, Cardiff Docks was shipping out more freight than any other port in the world.

In the meantime, other landowners had opened new mines and decided to strike deals of their own. New railway lines were opened to connect these mines with new docks at Penarth and Barry. Newport, which had valleys of its own to the north of it, became another thriving port. West of Barry there were yet more valleys, and these had coal, too, which was brought down on other railway lines, and then

shipped out from other ports – Port Talbot, Neath, Swansea and Llanelli. And so, within a few short years, the whole of South Wales became a blazing inferno of fire, steam and smoke, and blood, sweat and tears. And Cardiff was at the very heart of it.

Some say that all this activity brought 'prosperity'. Well, prosperity is relative. The real prosperity was felt by the landowners – the 'coal barons' as they became known – the railway tycoons, and the dock owners and shipowners. Some of these men became the multimillionaires of their day. The poor migrant workers who came to South Wales made a little money when times were good, and were perhaps better off than they had been when they had 'lived on the land'. But often, their cash was spent in shops cunningly owned by the coal owners, who paid their men in strange coinage that could only be spent in the company stores. And they rented small terraced cottages whose freehold was owned in perpetuity by the landowners.

There were many taverns where beer began to flow, and chapels were set up so that the men who drank in the taverns could come and feel a bit better about themselves on Sundays. Some of the men went to chapel, and some didn't. But the chapels later had a rival for the men's attentions, and that was the union lodge. 'Workers' rights' were won, amidst a furious background of strikes and lockouts. These pesky trade unionists – 'pesky' as far as the bosses were concerned – also set up things like hospitals and workingmen's clubs, with billiard rooms and libraries. Dangerous things, libraries!

That was the Valleys' towns. In Cardiff, too, there was a sudden mixture of Welsh, Irish, West Country and some Scottish people, packed together into cramped and insanitary housing blocks called 'slums'. They were employed in building the docks, and then working there, and working the railways. Later they also worked the steelworks (which was set up near Cardiff's coastline), breweries, and uncountable numbers of smaller foundries, engineering works and factories.

KING COAL

These days, Cardiff is a modern, vibrant city. It is home to a variety of national institutions, is a centre of learning and government, and regularly hosts major sporting and cultural events. There is a confidence about the place that, to those of us who spend much of our time in other Welsh towns, is almost tangible.

But it is a place that is in touch with its past. It knows the debt that it owes to others.

Cardiff developed into a major commercial centre during the nineteenth century. Its growth saw the construction of the Bute West Dock in 1839 (originally called the Bute Ship Canal), the Taff Vale Railway (1840) and the South Wales Railway a year later.

As any local schoolboy knows, this activity was almost entirely down to one factor: coal.

Cardiff grew rapidly from the 1830s onwards, when the Marquess of Bute built a dock that eventually linked to the Taff Vale Railway. Cardiff became the main port for exports of coal from the Valleys – between 1840 and 1870, coal production grew at a rate of nearly 80 per cent per decade. Much of this growth in productivity arose from workers being moved into the mining industry. Migration came from within and outside Wales: in 1851, a quarter of Cardiff's population were English-born, with many also being Irish-born. By the time of the 1881 census, Cardiff was the largest town in Wales.

Exports of coal and iron boomed as Cardiff's infrastructure stormed ahead to keep pace with it all. The second half of the nineteenth century saw a number of developments down by the docks, with the establishment of East Dock (1855), Roath Basin (1874) and then Roath Dock (1887).

The 1891 census records the population of Cardiff at almost 129,000 electors, but as that last decade of the century unfolded, the population grew by around 7,000 a year. Some 1,000 houses sprang up a year, alongside shops, schools and churches.

It's hard to understate the impact of the 'black gold' upon the development of the city. In 1899, Cardiff Docks exported around 8.5 million tons of coal, coke and patent fuel out of a total export and import trade of 11 million tons. So around 80 per cent of all exports from Cardiff Docks were made up of coal.

On 1 April 1995, the 'City Fathers' recognised the contribution made to the city by the miners, by awarding the freedom of Cardiff to the National Union of Mineworkers (South Wales Area). A fitting tribute indeed.

The transformation of Cardiff during the Industrial Revolution changed the nature of its population. As more and more people poured in from Ireland and England's West Country, the Welsh language was quickly all but obliterated by English. The accent changed, too, in this melting pot. What we were left with was a dialect that was less 'Caerdydd' and more, well, 'Kaairdiff' …

PUTTING THE ACCENT ON KAAIRDIFF

Some accents sound romantic. Some sound soothing. Some are made to welcome tourists.

The soft lilt of a sweet Irish Colleen, the friendly tones of a Geordie barmaid, or even the rat-a-tat tongue of a Scouse comic. All have their appeal.

But ours? Really?!

I get annoyed when people say that I 'don't sound Welsh'. To me, my sharp vowels and angular tones are just as Welsh as those of any Rhondda miner or Caernarfon cottage-burning nationalist.

But I know what they mean.

That Kaairdiff accent … well, it's not really that 'Welshy', I suppose. Not like the warm, sing-song lilt of, say, a Max Boyce (from Glynneath) or a Jonathan Davies (from Trimsaran).

Cardiff vowels are sharp and long. We say 'Car-Diff' or 'Pen-arth'. We call it Baaath Spaaa not Bawrth Spawh.

When imitated, it never really works. Nessa from Gavin and Stacey *is a great character, but we don't really talk like that. She is just a caricature. To hear a proper Cardiff accent, listen to Charlotte Church, Terry Holmes or Craig Bellamy. Or even Ali Yassine, the PA announcer at the Cardiff City Stadium. Stan Stennett (who is from Bridgend) didn't talk with a proper Cardiff accent, and even Frank Hennessy – a native Cardiffian, born and bred – 'puts it on' a little at times I think.*

As well as its distinctive sound, Cardiff talk is, like many other accents, littered with random use of words that add no real value to the dialogue. For example, a great many sentences end with the word 'like' or 'right' (pronounced 'rye', with the vowel sound dragged out for as long as possible). In a previous life, I used to man a housing-complaints hotline. So many calls would begin with 'rye, worri' is rye …' (Translation: 'Right, what it is, right …') I knew straight away that I was in for a hard time. The caller would often go on to explain how 'they gorra rehouse me, rye'. This is called glottalisation. That is, the 't' is hardly pronounced at all … rye.

When asking the whereabouts of something, a Cardiffian might ask, 'Where's that to?' The word 'to' adds no value to the sentence at all. It is a conversational quirk that has become almost an addiction to many Cardiffians.

Other words and letters also mutate, so 'huge' becomes 'yuge', 'ears' become 'years', human becomes 'yuman', and so on. A phrase such as Barry Island becomes 'Barrreee-eyelund'. A 'caravan at Barry Island' is almost pronounced as a single syllable. 'Cardiff Arms Park' is the quintessential example of the dialect at work.

The Cardiff talkers pretty much savage the Welsh language. In fact, place names such as Crwys and Llanedeyrn barely sound Welsh at all. 'Llanrumney', for instance, becomes 'Lan-rummy'. Why?!

The grammar also changes, bringing a tendency to – as a linguist would put it – use a third-person verb conjugation to describe a first/second person's actions. Thus, we say, 'I lives in Eleeee' rather than 'I live in Ely'.

However, we are unlikely to hear – sorry, year – 'I lives in Kingcoyd', for research has shown that there are social variations in the accent of standard English, compared with people from a working-class background. Thus, the city itself has different dialects, with people from, say,

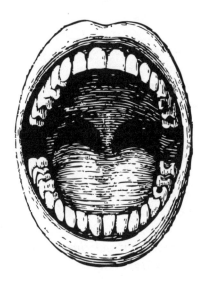

Llanrumney and Ely, having a stronger and broader accent than those living in Lisvane and Cyncoed.

This is why I say 'Claaaarks Pye' rather than 'Clahrkes Pie'. But this oddball accent of Cardiff's does not extend very far away from the city limits. Step east into the murky world of Newport, or even over the mountain to Caerphilly, and Charlotte Church sounds like a total foreigner. Cardiff people sometimes think that we are set apart from the rest of Wales. The unique accent does little to dispel this myth. And did you say 'apart' or 'apaaaaart' there by the way?

Quite why all this should be so is hard to decipher. It's probably down to the significant Irish influence in the growth of the city, with maybe a dash of West Country here and there. The Irishness can also be heard in the Scouse accent, reflecting the shared history of Cardiff and Liverpool as major westerly ports.

To close, here are some of my favourite examples of our unique tongue, with subtitles for the yard of earring – sorry 'hard of hearing':

I truly love my man.
I just loves him I do, rye …

Why does Juliette grieve so?
Wossamarrer wi' Dew Lee Ette?

Gosh Carl can be irritating.
Kaaaaal does my friggin' 'ed in.

Who will pay for these drinks?
Oooooze round is i'?

Are you off to the football match this weekend?
Yew going down the City sat dee?

What price are these goods, sir?
Ow much ar ease?

Four pounds – that sounds a little steep, if I may say so.
Fork kwid?! Strewth!

I'd like a pint of decent ale please.
S.A.

My car is in the garage.
My caaa zin the garidge.

Pardon?
Wah?

There is no dragon on the Union Flag, is there?
Why in we on the yunion jack?!

Do you take sugar?
Jew wan shuggur?

Whereabouts is that, exactly?
Where tooze at then?

And, my personal favourite …

To whom does that hat belong?
Ooze at is at?

2

FOOD
AND DRINK

As Cardiff was transformed from a sleepy little town into a hive of industry during the second half of the nineteenth century, more and more people were drawn to live here. The lifestyle of these newcomers was initially pretty haphazard, as there were no planned facilities for them. Scores of Irish navvies and their families were crammed into tiny terraced houses: fifty-four were discovered living in one four-bedroomed cottage in Cardiff, for instance. The living conditions were frequently awful.

Gradually the Corporation began to lay on decent facilities and to build better housing. Streets and districts were properly planned before they went up, instead of just developing randomly. Schools and hospitals were provided.

As life became less crazily hectic, the city's workers and their families began to settle down and consider how to spend their spare time. Where to go. What to do. And, before all that, what to eat – and drink.

Many of the beverages and food products that emerged during this period are delicacies peculiar to Cardiff. The taste also changes away from the city. Try them anywhere else and they just aren't the same!

CLARK'S PIES

A Clark's Pie.

The very words conjure up images of long, dark, terraced streets in Splott, Grangetown or Roath. Of dusty pints of Brains Beer or damp, open terraces.

The dish is woven into the very fabric of the city. As solid as the walls of Cardiff Castle.

The very name, 'Clark's Pie', is made for the Cardiff accent, almost impossible to pronounce without rasping out the vowel sound in your best 'broken-bottle' dialect. A Klaaaaark's Pie. About as Cardiff as it gets.

To describe it as 'just a pie' would be like saying that Fred Astaire 'could dance a bit' or that Usain Bolt was 'a bit nippy'. It is a self-contained feast with a smell, weight and texture all of its own.

The history of the Clark's Pie goes back to the early years of the twentieth century. It began in a bakery in Donald Street, Roath, where one Mary Clark began to put together the wholesome product. By 1928, a larger bakehouse was erected to respond to demand, and the operation moved to Paget Street in Grangetown.

Mary Clark was truly a piewoman extraordinaire. She had seven children, all of whom followed her into the pie trade. Several of them ended up running similar pie shops in Newport, Bristol, Gloucester, Swindon and Reading. The Cardiff business expanded, opening another shop in Canton, near Victoria Park, in 1913.

Mary's son Arthur had the idea of registering the 'CLARPIE' trademark in 1934. This trademark is still stamped – 'branded', perhaps – into the bottom of every Clark's Original Pie today. The Paget Street shop – the very nerve centre of the Clark's Pie operation – moved to nearby Bromsgrove Street, Grangetown, in 1955, under the supervision of Mary's grandson Dennis Dutch. It continues there to this day.

In 2012, the trusty pie was in the news for all the wrong reasons – as two sides of Cardiff's famous pie-making family became involved in a major dispute.

The two bakeries run by the descendants of Mary Clark came into conflict when the owners of the Canton 'Clark's Pie' shop decided to rebrand their operation as the 'Victoria Park Pie Company'. The owners of the Grangetown bakery, however, did not want the famous branded pies sold under any other name than Clark's.

Even Cardiff Council Trading Standards officials became embroiled. The 'pie wars' were now threatening to destabilise a veritable city institution! However, all has now been resolved, and the main thing to remember is that Clark's Pies are just as tasty as ever. And the Victoria Park pies are not bad either.

In a former life I worked on the food outlets at Ninian Park – the former home of Cardiff City FC. At 10 a.m. on every other Saturday, seventy-two cold pies would be delivered to our unit beneath the grandstand, so I could warm them up slowly, ready for the masses to enjoy in the traditional sporting surroundings. Outlets all around the stadium would receive similar deliveries. We would easily sell all seventy-two pies, of course. Or rather, seventy-one. Mysteriously, one would always go down as 'waste' and somehow find its way into my hands for later.

One Saturday, we were playing Norwich City. After the game, we had closed down our unit, swept the floor, balanced the books and so on, and then headed out to the front of the stadium to drop off our aprons. At the same time, Delia Smith – the famous TV cook, who is also the owner of Norwich City – was coming out of the main reception and was about to climb into her Range Rover. I seized the moment. Reaching under my overall, I elegantly proffered this most delectable of Cardiff delicacies. With great subtlety and aplomb, I attempted to gently introduce her to its manifold charms.

'Jew wanna pie?!' I yelled.

Delia regarded me as if I had crawled out from under a stone. To say that she looked 'down her nose' at me wouldn't even come close to it. She did not, it seems, want a pie.

'You don't know what you're missing girl!'

The exact recipe of the pie is virtually a state secret. It is as closely guarded as the formula for Coca-Cola. Yes, there is beef, some onions and a thick gravy-type substance, but there is also – what is that taste? Is it pepper? Is it paprika? Is it iron ore from the former East Moors steelworks? Nobody really knows.

These magic feasts are cooked fresh each day and delivered to retail outlets direct from the pie shops. They comprise a thick, almost dusty pastry, which negates the need for cutlery entirely. A connoisseur will bite a hole in the end, pour in tomato – or even brown – sauce and munch the whole lot from his bare hands. No washing up or serviette is called for. It is total food.

In local parts, it is considered an act of treason to freeze or (heaven forbid) microwave these beautiful creatures. They are warmed up gently, as one might woo a beautiful woman, before gazing into her pastry eyes and – mmmmmm.

Just a pie? Yeah, right.

Okay, now we have all had our pie, we are going to want to wash it down with something ...

IT'S BRAINS YOU WANT!

Brains Beers is the ultimate family brewery.

Able to trace its origins back more than 200 years, its history reads like a narrative of the city itself. Samuel Arthur Brain served as Lord Mayor of Cardiff as long ago as 1899–1900, when the troops were pulling on pints of 'Light' and 'Daark' before setting off for the relief of Mafeking.

Since Samuel – old S.A. himself – there have been other notable figures in the dynasty. Michael Brain, for instance, who managed to resist the march of the big national breweries in the 1960s and keep Brains independent; and Christopher Brain, who oversaw the transfer of the brewery from St Mary Street to the modernised Penarth Road site, ensuring the brewery was ready for the challenges of the new millennium.

Brains' ales and branding have entered the lexicon of our streets. Samuel Arthur's initials live on in the famous 'S.A.' best bitter, which has entered the Cardiff vocabulary. Brains S.A. is the only beer I know to have a nickname: 'Skull Attack', in tribute to the strength of this mighty ale; or even – we are talking the 1970s now – 'Steve Austin', a reference, presumably, to the 'bionic' powers it gave you, just like Steve Austin, TV's Bionic Man. Not sure about that one.

Brains have been responsible for some iconic adverts over the years. 'It's Brains You Want!' used to be splashed across the top of Cardiff double-decker buses, and, of course, on railway bridges. The visual effect of this was so impressive that the Super Furry Animals used it to

illustrate the sleeve notes of their 1996 debut album Fuzzy Logic. *The Brains brand was marketed on Cardiff City football shirts in the '90s, and, in the noughties, on Wales rugby jerseys.*

There are many other fine examples of local beers in South Wales: Tomos Watkin is growing in popularity, Rhymney beers boast a distinct local quality, and I still have an affection for Allbright – the beer of my youth. But no other beer really cries 'Caaardiff' in the way that a thick pint of Brains does.

Now, it would be so easy to fill the rest of these pages with reminiscences of former Brains pubs that are no more. The giant Grosvenor in Splott (once reputed to be the biggest Brains pub in the world), the tiny Taff Vale – when there were still pubs to be found in Queen Street – or the York at the top of Butetown on Canal Wharf. All these landmarks were home to the famed dusty brew. Thick pints of creamy light or dark beer, overflowing to dampen beer mats as it washed down a lunchtime pasty.

But this is largely an image of a world that no longer exists. When was the last time you bought a pasty in a pub? Or saw an old man in a cloth cap pulling on a battered cigarette over a pint of dark? Hmm, indeed. So is Brains brewery itself just a memento of Cardiff's industrial past? Is the old family firm about to drift away into history alongside the Custom House or the North and South in Louisa Street?

Not a bit of it. In 2007, this famous Cardiff company celebrated 125 years of brewing. And, whilst remembering its proud heritage, Brains remains as much a part of the new Cardiff as it was of the old.

Having launched a rebranding of its famous dragon logo in 2003, Brains introduced innovative and witty advertising campaigns to support its links with the Welsh Rugby Union in 2005. We have also seen links with cricket and international football develop alongside new innovations such as smooth beer, satellite TV and Sunday lunches. They even own a coffee shop. All have been embraced by Brains as the old firm has survived and prospered into the new millennium. Brains has shed its 'cloth-cap' image, whilst still remaining true to its roots. As central to Cardiff as St Mary Street itself.

Makes you fancy a pint, doesn't it?

The problem is, once you have eaten your Clark's Pie and washed it down with a few pints of Brains, you are sometimes left wanting more. The thirst has been slaked, but then the hunger comes on again. Time, then, to try out another of Cardiff's culinary delights.

HALF AND HALF

Now this one has me beat.

There is no reason I can recall, research, or even invent why this dish should be aligned so closely with the capital city.

But for some reason, the simple combination of a large plate – of which half is covered in chips and half houses the rice, all smothered in a curry sauce of indifferent quality – has become synonymous with Cardiff catering.

Critical analysis of the dish is almost pointless. It comprises simply rice, chips and curry. There may be some limp mango chutney, and perhaps a poppadom or two. This is all collectively referred to as simply 'Half and Half'. The phrase carries universal understanding from the furthest outreaches of Ely to the darkest corners of Trowbridge. When Charlotte Church brings out a celebrity chef cookbook, this will be recipe number one, for sure.

About 5 miles down the road in Newport, it is unheard of. There they have their 'Cheese and Chips', but in the works canteens of the Big City it's arffff an arffff every time luv.

Now this leads us on to where you would eat your 'arff an arff'. Where would you procure it, and where would you consume it? Simples. If you were doing the weekend 'tour of Cardiff' thing and wanted to sample a genuine cultural 'flavour of the city', then there is no more characteristic place to go for both procurement and consumption of this delightful dish than the exotic shangri-la that is Caroline Street.

SWEET CAROLINE

Caroline Street. Beauty or Beast?

When first discussing the concept of this book, our publishers were keen to ensure that we uncovered all the quirky, charming little oddities that make our city so appealing.

For the 'Food and Drink' section, they pictured vivid descriptions of quaint Llandaff tearooms and evocative portraits of Pontcanna bistros. We would recreate the delicate delight of cream teas in David Morgan's cafeteria, perhaps?

Nah …

We can do better than that.

Caroline Street has always enjoyed something of an uncertain reputation. Like a stain on the sofa that won't go away, no matter how much you rearrange the cushions.

When I first began to venture into town on the Saturday mornings of my adolescence, Caroline Street's claim to fame lay in the number of outlets from whence it was possible to buy 'dirty books'. Pornography, if you will.

Back in those pre-Internet days, the only way to locate 'porn' was to go and find it in the woods. This worked rather more times than you might expect, to be honest, and my teenage years often featured trips to the scruffier, overgrown 'mouse fields' of Tremorfa in search of lusty fiction hidden away by some degenerate or other.

So, to discover a street that housed shops which actually traded in such material gave Caroline Street a notoriety and an 'edge' that it probably retains to this day.

Quite who 'Caroline' was, or why she became worthy of immortalisation in the city's street-naming system, is unclear. The strongest claim to its provenance may come from Caroline of Brunswick, the wife of George IV. Whoever it was named after, it became a focal point of the cultural life of the city centre. By day a haven for mackintosh-wearing old men and furtive teenagers; by night, a refuge for drunken revellers, teetering into the many 'chippies' to seek sustenance after an evening of boozing. Caroline Street, in my 20s, became the place for me to dine out in Cardiff.

Alright, 'dine' may be stretching a point, but certainly many a long, boozy night in the pubs and clubs of the capital have ended up with a visit to this famous little thoroughfare, which runs from St Mary Street to the Hayes. Plenty of restaurants and takeaways. Chips with everything if you really want it, but for me, there is only one dish of choice in this gourmet's ghetto.

'Off the bone.'

I was in Newport on a night out once (not recommended) and, inevitably, ended my evening at a local chippie. Imagine my shock to be told by the proprietor, at around 10 p.m., that they had 'run out' of curry sauce. 'You would go out of business if you ran out of curry sauce in Cardiff,' I helpfully pointed out.

'Off the bone', or – to use the Latin – chicken-curry-off-the-bone-with-chips – is available from Dorothy's, which I consider to be the best of the Caroline Street takeaways. To describe it as the House Special would be an understatement. It is the ultimate signature dish.

The dish consists of white-hot chips, strips of gleaming white, crumbly chicken, and what can seem like a deep ladle-full of thick curry sauce. The sauce may be orange, or it may be brown. Who knows. But at 2 a.m., it is the very manna from heaven. The joys of walking through the cold night air shovelling forkfuls of this delicacy down you have to be experienced first-hand.

Dorothy's (formerly Dorothy's Fish Bar), dates back to 1953. Its place at the heart of the many takeaways to have occupied this tiny terrace down the years is secure. It remains one of the longest-established premises of its type in the whole city. And just in case you were wondering, that's a '5' I spotted on the 'scores on the doors' food hygiene ratings by the way (site visit: 23 December 2013!).

These days, there are those who would spruce up Caroline Street and merge it with the city's ever-growing 'Cafe Quarter'. The old, simple charm of the place would soon disappear beneath the new paving, the clutch of bistros, the encroaching 'tapas bars' and revamped pubs at either end of the street – the 'march of progress', dear boy.

But Caroline Street soldiers on. Sweet Caroline is still hanging in there, offering nourishment amidst the midnight mayhem, still the last word in countless diary entries, recording the many, many nights she has helped draw to a close.

Bless her.

Right, we have had our night out now. Clark's Pie, Brains beers and then Caroline Street. Enough already. Let's say, though, you had a real monster of a session: all-day boozing, and Caroline Street was just the 'half-time' nosh-up. Where would you go then, when you got the munchies, after the 'final whistle' – or, as they tend to say in pubs, at 'closing time'? Well, you can't do this now, but in the old days …

THE PATRICE WAS EVRA SO GOOD …

Now I just know that many of you out there will be turning misty-eyed at the very mention of these words. You will be taken back to your youth. To days of promises made in the heat of the night, of rushing home before it got too light. Blaming it on the wine – but always still stopping at 'Patsies' for the ultimate late-night meal.

I first visited The Patrice Grill – to give it its full, glorious name – in September 1974. To a slightly unworldly 15-year-old, it seemed as though I had been shown a glimpse of Heaven itself. In the coming years, as I stumbled through my stormy teens towards the calmer waters of my mid-20s and 30s, it became almost a second home.

Cardiffians who enjoyed their young days in the '70s will recall many an exotic name as we took our steps out into the city's nightlife: Tito's, The Top Rank, The Cavern, Bakers Row, Monties, the Dowlais, and a score of other salubrious venues. All these nocturnal arenas of pleasure played their part in my adventures, but The Patrice was the daddy of them all.

This late-night cafe-cum-restaurant was the sort of place which simply does not exist these days. My 21-year-old son respects the beauty of Caroline Street, and can also do battle with the best kebabs that City Road has to offer. But he is in awe at my stories of Patsies.

The place opened at 10 p.m., as I recall. A glass-fronted establishment located at No. 14 Clifton Street. Officially this is Roath, but it always felt more like Adamsdown to me. Opposite was Roath Police Station. Convenient, I always thought.

In its halcyon days of the mid-'70s, the place would become so crowded that there could be half an hour's wait before a table became free. There was no bar, or indeed any other form of waiting area. Hungry revellers would simply line the spaces between the tables, standing and waiting eagerly for a group of diners to finish their meals and vacate. No booking, no reservations, no preferential treatment. But the system knew who was next, and the laws of the jungle prevented any queue jumping. If you took a bird to this place, chances are you either never saw her again, or she remains at your side to this day.

And the food. Oh, the food.

Over the years, I think we covered the whole menu. The steaks, the gammons, chicken, even grilled trout at 4 a.m. one hazy Sunday. The Patrice was distinctly parochial in its cuisine – their menu's notion of 'continental dishes' extended simply to three types of curry (distinguished as chicken, beef or prawn – none of your madras, vindaloo and what-have-you) and spaghetti bolognese. Trust me, these dishes were considered 'cosmopolitan' in The Patrice.

But our favourite was the pork chop. I feel sorry for the modern generation, weaned on Dial-A-Pizza and Chicken Buckets. They will never know the joy of a huge pork chop,

mountains of thin chips, a dull clump of peas and an extra 'splash' of curry sauce (10p!).

*This was no place for the meek or the faint-hearted. No room for subtlety either, as the menu announced in bold type. 'All meals must be paid for on delivery.' None of this namby-pamby 'may we have the bill now?' nonsense. At The Patrice, you paid your cash **before** you ate the grub – or you didn't get the grub. End of.*

Like many of us who hail from east of the city centre, I have countless stories from The Patrice. The fellow reveller who once coolly pinched a policeman's hat during a raid. Or the indescribable scenes as that famed local 'character', the giant 'Nosher', once tried to steal the fat from the plate of a certain future author! The unique hygiene of the toilets. I even once proposed to the slightly sturdy waitress Pam, who woke me after I had nodded off waiting for my meal (as you do!). As I opened my eyes, the sight which greeted me was a giant chop with all the above trimmings. Ecstasy! 'Will you marry me, Pam?' I said. 'Course I will love, course I will.'

It has closed down now, I am afraid. Part of me misses the place, but part of me smiles at the fact that is a part of my life that is no more. Locked away in the sock drawer of my memories. My fellow revellers all now grey or grampies. Memories of days and nights when … there just seemed less to worry about.

It sounds like quite a place! Now, it could be complained that most of the pleasures that have been assembled in this chapter – drinking beer, eating takeaways – are part of the 'old' Cardiff. Of cloth-capped workmen drinking their pints of dark, fag in hand, in a dusty corner of a spit-and-sawdust pub.

But David, who has penned all of this evocative stuff, is not just a man for harking back to the Cardiff of old. He is also very much a man of Cardiff 'new'. Here he takes a look at dining in today's shiny new city.

CAFE SOCIETY

Many of the eating houses, pubs and even the food itself, which are described elsewhere in this book, portray a certain 'image' of Cardiff, perhaps. Of life 'south of the Railway Line' or, as Frank Hennessy once wrote, 'Cardiff after Dark'. A clever line.

But the modern city, whilst proud of its traditions and industrial origins, is not all chips and thick beer. These days, areas such as Mill Lane, St David's 2 and Cardiff Bay all play host to an international smörgåsbord of cafes, restaurants and assorted other cosmopolitan places-to-be-seen-in. All culture is truly here, if only we look hard enough. We can find, for instance, a tapas bar in Caroline Street, close to a Thai restaurant and a clutch of trendy wine bars. St Mary Street offers a Portuguese diner, whilst there are even places in the city where you can buy sushi these days.

Yet, even in these continental quarters, pockets of swish 'Welshness' can also be located by the determinedly discerning.

Cadwaladers, for instance, is a family run chain of cafes that originated in Criccieth (Caernarfonshire). The first parlour was created by David and Hannah Cadwalader in, appropriately enough, 1927. (Any readers unsure about the significance of 1927, please proceed to the far wall for despatch by firing squad. Alternatively, read the Cardiff City piece in our Sporting Cardiff chapter.)

After Dafydd Cadwalader died in 1983, Cadwalader's was purchased by a family of Welsh entrepreneurs, the Andrews family, who also own Castle Leisure (they have a premises on Newport Road by the way). The owners expanded the business to cover the whole of North Wales and, eventually, Cardiff.

The Cadwaladers cafe in Mermaid Quay is typical of the modern city. Delicacies on offer include Hannah

Cadwalader's secret recipe vanilla ice cream, a variety of other luxuriously flavoured ice creams, lunch items and coffee products (including a specially developed exclusive blend of espresso), intoxicating hot chocolate and loose-leaf tea. Not a tea bag in sight here. To describe these treats as mere food and drink would border on the insulting.

The modern city centre and Cardiff Bay are liberally sprinkled with these elegant new examples of how to dine in style. The crockery has a Continental feel to it, while the decor is wood, slate and glass. It feels like Milan, not Mill Lane.

These establishments set the agenda for catering in the new millennium. Fresh-faced baristas take customer care to new levels, serving skinny latte to on-the-go media types. Beautiful people relax on sofas while 'scores on the doors' Food Hygiene Ratings offer up-front reassurances that dining here is safe. Indeed, it feels almost compulsory.

That completes our odyssey through the delights of Cardiff catering. To finish the chapter, here is a completely random addition – one of those lists that just had to go in the book somewhere. So here it is …

PUBS IN THE 'WRONG' STREETS

Lots of pubs in the Cardiff of my youth seemed to have been given the 'wrong' names. (Or they had the right name, but had been put in the 'wrong' street!) What I mean to say is, many pub-goers noticed that the name of the pub was not consistent with the street in which it was located. Anyway, read the list and it should make sense.

1. **The Wyndham** *(Canton)*
This characterful pub, once popular with Irish labourers, closed in the late '80s, and is now an office of some kind. But why was it called the Wyndham? Wyndham Crescent, Wyndham Road and Wyndham Street are all nearby, round a couple of corners. But the pub was in none of these streets. It stood on the corner of Cowbridge Road East and Wellington Street. Wouldn't it have been less confusing to have called it The Wellington?

2. The Craddock *(Canton or Grangetown? – not sure)*
Not far from Craddock Street – but again, not in it. The Craddock was on the other side of Ninian Park Road from the Craddock Street turning.

3. The Insole *(Canton)*
Nowhere near Insole Court, which is in Llandaff.

4. The Duke of Clarence *(Canton)*
Nowhere near Clarence Road, which is in Grangetown.

5. The Radyr Court *(Danescourt)*
This one is not even in the right area. It's in Danescourt, not Radyr (which no longer even has a pub). Although historians will point out that the pub is where the original manor house of Radyr – 'Radyr Court' – actually stood.

6. The New Ely *(Cathays)*

Another pub which is the wrong area altogether. It's not in Ely, it's in Cathays. It was called 'The New Ely' because it was an Ely Ales pub. So when the brewery first opened it, it was indeed 'the new Ely' pub. (This confused a fellow (journalism) student of mine twenty years ago, who was from Bristol. He had heard about the Ely riots, but – having wandered around the vicinity of The New Ely pub – he declared that he 'couldn't understand the rioters' because, in his opinion, there was 'nothing too bad' about the area.) P.S. It's not called The New Ely anymore, it's called something else. Don't ask me what.

7. The Neville *(Grangetown)*

Not in Neville Street, which is about half a mile away, but on the corner of Clare Road and Court Road.

8. The Gower *(Cathays)*

Close to Gower Street, but actually it stood in Gwennyth Road – on the opposite side of the road from the Gower Street turning.

9. The Albany *(Roath)*

Just on the other side of the railway line from the Gower (now closed) was The Albany (still open). This is in the back-streets north of Albany Road but it isn't *in* Albany Road, it's in Donald Street.

10. The Mackintosh *(Cathays)*

Not *too* far from Mackintosh Place, Roath, but actually in Mundy Place in neighbouring Cathays.

Yes, there are other more obvious ones, too, when you come to think of it: Plymouth Arms (St Fagans) isn't in Plymouth, and the Murrayfield (Pentwyn) was nowhere near Edinburgh ... etc., etc.

Before anyone writes in to say I am being stupid, I realise that many of these pubs were named after local landowning families – your Wyndhams, Nevilles and Insoles – and that the streets were named after the same people. Still, it makes a tidy Top Ten, dunnit?

Addition: streets given the 'wrong' name
Wyndham Crescent, in Canton, is a road. It has a slightly looping shape, but it is not, by any stretch of the imagination, a crescent. Wyndham Road is a crescent that runs off Wyndham Crescent, forms a crescent and then runs back into Wyndham Crescent.

So surely, Wyndham Crescent should have been Wyndham Road and Wyndham Road should have been Wyndham Crescent? Did the Corporation workmen make a mistake with the street signs when they put them up all those years ago?

Sorry to have raised what must seem like an absolutely inconsequential issue, but this thing has been bugging me for thirty years.

3

CIVIC
SOCIETY

THE BIRTH OF A CITY

Throughout the nineteenth century, Cardiff grew in population at a breakneck pace. Initially, there was little in the way of
'town planning' and slums sprouted up at random around the
'Old Town' by the castle. There was Crockherbtown (a strange
spelling: the place was normally pronounced 'Crockerton'),
which sprouted up just to the east of the Old Town. This area
is now commemorated in the name of Crockherbtown Lane,
which runs behind Queen Street. Between the Old Town
and the docks, the tight-knit communities of Newtown and
Butetown sprang up. Finally, in the area bounded by Cardiff
General railway station, the River Taff, the rugby stadium and
St Mary Street, there was Temperance Town. Nearly all of
these areas no longer exist, razed to the ground in successive
waves of slum clearance in more recent times.

Cardiff grew first, then, in fairly higgledy-piggledy and
random fashion. It was a similar story in the other great
industrial cities of Britain: Birmingham, Nottingham,
Sheffield, Leeds, Newcastle, Manchester, Liverpool and
Glasgow. Gradually, as Britain grew richer, better facilities
began to be introduced in these towns – partly as a result
of philanthropic social reform, and partly due to pressure

exerted on Parliament by workers' movements (the trade unions, the Lib/Lab wing of the Liberal Party, and then the Labour Party).

In Cardiff, as in these other great industrial towns, improvements were gradually made. But for the councilmen of Cardiff (known as the Cardiff Corporation) to be able to provide anything in the way of better facilities, they first had to take legal control of the town, most of which, by the 1870s, was beyond the bounds of the old city walls.

The Cardiff Improvement Act of 1875 saw the Corporation take charge of the 'virtual towns' that had sprung up around Cardiff. Roath, on the east side of the town centre, and Canton, on the west side, were incorporated into the town. Cardiff became – for the first time – the largest town or city in Wales, overtaking Merthyr. In 1888, it was recognised as a county borough, meaning that the Cardiff Corporation was responsible for providing all the major facilities in the town.

Industry continued apace. The Coal Exchange opened in Mount Stuart Square, near the docks, in 1886. This was the late-Victorian equivalent of a trade centre, a place where coal barons, shipowners and bankers met to do deals. The world's first £1 million cheque was signed there in 1904. The Merthyr iron-owners opened a major steelworks in Cardiff, close to the docks (the East Moors works), in 1891.

The fourth and largest of the Bute Docks was opened – by King Edward VII, no less – in 1907. Then, in 1913, Cardiff reached its peak as a coal-exporting harbour, with 10 million tons of the black gold being shipped out – making it the busiest port in the world.

The docks were where the big money was being made: this was the financial centre of Cardiff. Around the 'Old Town' of the castle, two new centres emerged: a retail and leisure centre of shops and market stalls, pubs, theatres, dance halls and, later, cinemas, centred upon Queen Street, the Hayes, St Mary Street, Castle Street and Westgate Street; and a civic centre located just north of the castle.

In 1898, the Corporation purchased – from the Marquess of Bute – an area known as Cathays Park as the site of this new civic centre. Between then and the First World War, they built the City Hall, the Law Courts, the University of Wales Registry, the Glamorgan County Hall, parts of the Technical College, and the foundations of the National Museum of Wales. Not a bad enterprise, considering that Cardiff was still only a town when this project was first undertaken. During the time it was under construction – perhaps not coincidentally – Cardiff, in 1905, became a city.

Cardiff possessed other strong claims for city status, apart from the Civic Centre. The Free Library had opened near St John's church in 1882 (this is now 'the Old Library'). The University College had been founded in 1893. At around the same time, William Burges, the architect and medievalist, was renovating the castle. The 'Castle Grounds' were purchased as part of this scheme.

Other crucial services had also been provided; facilities that we would now take for granted. In 1885, the Cardiff Corporation became the first council in Wales to provide its town with an electricity supply. The generating station was at Eldon Road (later renamed Ninian Park Road).

What nobody knew then was that bad times were just around the corner. Almost as soon as the last shot was fired in the First World War, Cardiff began to decline. The 1920s saw oil replacing coal as the fuel for ships, which meant much less demand for Welsh steam coal. To add to this problem, the best of the Welsh coal seams had already been 'worked out' from the mines by this time.

The economy of Cardiff slumped. Unemployment in the city reached a dismal 25 per cent in 1930. However, by mentioning this decline I am 'getting ahead of myself' a bit.

Because the following chapter is all about the emergence of Cardiff as a major city, and the amenities and facilities which developed as it was transformed from a grubby, ramshackle, busy little town, into a prestigious, statuesque and oh-so-modern city.

GOING BACK TO MY ROUTES

Transport in the City

Cardiff has been used as a transport 'hub' – to use a modern term – since ancient times. Initially, the River Taff was the main route in and out of the city. Dan O'Neill, the long-serving *South Wales Echo* columnist, quotes evidence that the Vikings used Cardiff as a trading post back in the ninth century. The Norse pirates had vessels of up to 200 tons sailing up the river (in what is now Westgate Street), carried along by 12ft of water at high tides. However, the river was only navigable for a fairly short distance, barely much further north than Canton Bridge.

Later, the problem of north-south transportation into Cardiff was solved by building an artificial 'river', the Glamorganshire Canal, alongside the Taff (in around 1800). Within fifty years, there was so much coal needing to be brought down to Cardiff Docks from the Valleys, that the canal was no longer a viable option. So the Taff Vale Railway was built as a third north–south transport system. Then, eventually, we had the A470 dual carriageway built alongside *that* – although part of the A470 (North Road and Caerphilly Road) ran along the route of the original old Roman road north to Caerphilly.

The need to build railway lines through the city centre meant that the Taff had to be diverted, to prevent the lines from being regularly flooded. By the 1860s, the river had been straightened and Cardiff's original quay area had disappeared, to be replaced by the newly built Westgate Street.

So much for the north–south routes, but what about east–west routes? Well, the first one was the old Roman road from Caerleon to Neath, which is basically the original blueprint for the A48, including Newport Road, Queen Street and Cowbridge Road, East and West. That road was upgraded (in around 1800) into a mail-coach road (and parts of it were also turnpike roads).

Then, with the coming of the steam trains, we had the arrival of the South Wales Railway, which connected Chepstow to Swansea, in 1850. A couple of years later, this route became somewhat more useful when it connected to the Great Western Railway (GWR) line, which went from Gloucester to London. GWR's engineer Isambard Kingdom Brunel made this connection possible by supervising the building of the Chepstow Bridge over the River Wye. The GWR, which was becoming one of Britain's biggest companies, then took over the South Wales Railway following a merger in 1862.

Despite the building of the Chepstow Bridge, logistical problems remained. The Chepstow Bridge only spanned the Wye, which meant the trains still had to go all the way 'up and around' Gloucester, because a much bigger river – the Severn – was in the way. The GWR solved that problem – after a lot of trouble – by completing the Severn Tunnel in 1886. Cardiff now linked directly with Paddington, without passengers having to go via Gloucester. Within a few years, the journey time for this route had been reduced to just under three hours and 'Cardiff General', all poshed up nicely by the GWR, had become the place where visitors took their first glimpse of the city of Cardiff.

(If you are wondering what happened to the Chepstow Bridge, the Severn Tunnel emerged on the 'Wales' side of the Severn, west of Chepstow and **west of the River Wye** – so from 1886, the Chepstow Bridge was completely bypassed.

The train no longer had to cross the River Wye. If you are still confused – as I was – check out the route of the railway line on a map. However, the Chepstow Bridge – albeit restructured in 1962 – is still there, and you will cross it if you are journeying by train from Cardiff to Gloucester. Or if you are going to London on a Sunday and you are diverted via Gloucester, as often happens.)

As rail services improved, train journeys became a veritable pleasure. Alan Price-Talbot of Caerphilly remembers travelling to London for the first time (in the 1930s) in a train made up of corridor coaches pulled by the gleaming green-and-gold King George V steam locomotive. Afternoon tea was served, comprised of buttered toasted tea cakes and pastries, served by gentlemen waiters dressed in short, white mess jackets, with 'GWR chocolate' (as it was known) coloured trousers. On arrival at Paddington, the driver leaned out of his footplate to accept the thanks of passengers for their safe journey – some of whom handed him cigarettes as a form of a tip!

In the late 1950s, with rail about to be superseded by road – or so we were told by Dr Beeching – the M4 began to be constructed. In 1966, the section from the newly built Severn Bridge to Junction 18 opened. Over the next twenty-five years, the sections west of Cardiff to Carmarthenshire were built.

Motor traffic had increased six-fold during the 1920s, and this led to a sharp need for better roads within the city. Leslie Hore-Belisha, the Transport Minister – he of the 'Belisha beacon' – opened the new Leckwith Road Bridge in 1935. Another major project, in the pre-motorway era, was the opening of the Western Avenue in 1939.

Thirty years later, the Gabalfa flyover began operating (officially known as Gabalfa Interchange, but everyone calls it 'the flyover'). It is difficult, though, to pinpoint when exactly Culverhouse Cross began, as this junction – in my youth, just a small roundabout – mushroomed and became more and more gargantuan over the years!

As well as allowing more and more people to zoot around the city in their cars, these roads also allowed for the improvement of public transport within Cardiff.

Horses for Courses

The first **public transport** provided by the Cardiff Corporation came in 1872, in the shape of horse buses. These were basically a public transport version of the horse-and-carriage affairs owned by rich people for their private transportation.

We already had the long-distance mail-coach routes, such as Cardiff (the Angel Hotel) to Cowbridge (the Bear Hotel). The first horse-bus routes within the city were from Cardiff Castle (or the Angel) to Llandaff North. In the 1870s, Cathedral Road had not yet been built (it was still merely a lane), so the route would have been along Cowbridge Road East through Canton, then up Llandaff Road. There were later variations, such as Severn Grove–Mortimer Road–Conway Road. The route continued to go through Canton, as this was a populous area, where many passengers would be picked up. The route terminated by the Cow and Snuffers pub.

Horses provided the main form of public transport in Cardiff for many years. As well as the Corporation horse buses, we had horse-cabs run by David Moore from Anglesey Street in Canton for forty years (1880–1920), and wagonettes – fifteen-seater affairs – run by James Redway from nearby Lewis Court, behind Woolworths in Canton, in the early years of the century. The Angel Hotel was a major terminal for these services.

Even after other forms of transport were introduced, horse-drawn vehicles were still regularly seen on the roads of Cardiff until well after the Second World War. But eventually, as more and more cars and motor buses (what we now call 'buses') proliferated, they all but disappeared.

Tram-endous Stuff

There was an early flirtation with another horse-drawn form of transport called a 'horse tram'. The word 'tram' suggests tramways, grooves made in the roads so that steel carriages could run along the grooves. In industry, some hills had been too steep for horses to easily pull cartloads of freight up them – because wooden wheels will tend to roll back on a gradient. It was discovered that metal wheels, running along a groove, offered more resistance to the hill and so horse trams began to be used to shift cargo. They were first used to take limestone from the quarries of the Mumbles to Swansea Docks; in 1807, this was turned into a service to take passengers along the same route.

It was some time before the horse trams took off, though. They were trialled in New York in the 1830s, and, in the 1860s, the council in Toronto allowed them to start taking over from horse buses as the main form of public transport. In Britain, Birkenhead followed suit; and in 1878, so did Cardiff, but here they operated alongside the existing horse buses and never took over from them. They did, however, lead to the laying down of the first tramways in the city.

By the turn of the century, the idea of horse trams began to look obsolete, as a new thing called 'electricity' had been discovered. In 1902, electric trams came in to replace the horse trams. On 1 May, the Mayor of Cardiff 'drove' the first tram from the city centre, through Canton and then along Cathedral Road.

The trams ran in grooves on the road (in which cyclists' wheels could become stuck), with overhead wiring conducting the electrical power. One of the main routes was the 'Parks Express', which ran between Roath Park and Victoria Park. These parks were where the tramways came to an end (or 'terminated'), and so they were known as 'terminals'. Another terminus was in St Mary Street, hence 'The Terminus' pub, and another was by the Royal Oak pub on Newport Road.

The trams immediately took off, and within a year, the Corporation had replaced all of its horse-tram services with the newfangled electric ones.

The trams' domination was not to last for too long, though. Within three decades, the Corporation was flirting with the next new thing: trolleybuses. However, the trams certainly died a lingering death, as tram services continued until 1950.

Eventually, the trams were replaced by the trolleybuses, which, like the trams, had overhead wiring for the electricity but, crucially, ran on the road using normal tyres, instead of running on tramways.

Off Their Trolleys
There can be few, if any, images that cry out 'Cardiff' as loudly as the old trolleybuses.

These giant purple-and-yellow monsters could have stumbled straight from the set of Dr Who. *Enormous, space-age creations that rumbled all over the city in a Dalek-type invasion.*

But their arrival predates the introduction of the eternal Time Lord to our fair city by some distance. The trolleybus dates back to 1901, when the first passenger-carrying system began operating near Dresden in Germany. Leeds and Bradford were the first British cities to introduce a similar service, in 1911. Within the next few years, fifty different councils in Britain opted to go for trolleybus systems, with the biggest network being in London.

Initially, the idea was that, as cities expanded outwards, trolleybus services would be introduced as extensions to the existing tram routes. This would save councils the expense of having to extend the tramlines – which, in Cardiff, never went beyond Victoria Park in the west, and Roath Park and the Royal Oak in the east of the city.

In 1934, the City Corporation decided to gradually introduce trolley vehicles. These devilish devices would utilise the existing overhead electrical equipment – giant poles connecting the buses eerily to overhead wires – making the finished article look like some enormous toy train set brought in by the gods to amuse themselves.

St David's Day (1 March) 1942 saw the first of these magnificent beasts adorn our streets, as the whole of the old tramway system began its conversion to trolleybuses. The buses utilised a unique fare system, with a single penny allowing passengers to travel any distance. No ticket, no change, just chuck your penny in that box there. This saw Cardiff bus users enjoying among the lowest fares in Britain, for a time.

Each bus was staffed by a driver and a conductor. You couldn't get on at the front, and the conductor's role was to supervise payment and control the platform. That 'platform' was a kind of deck at the end of the bus, which led to the open entrance. There was no door. If you were cunning enough, it enabled you to hop off the bus in between stops *if it suited – though this was frowned upon. It worked the other way, too, of course – allowing desperate chases to leap on board as the giant vehicle snaked away from the bus stop.*

However, by the '60s, trolleybuses were themselves being overtaken by petrol-fuelled motorised buses – basically, the kind of buses we have today. Motor buses didn't need any overhead wires or poles, so transport planners could introduce new routes – and vary existing ones – much more easily. Trolleybus services in Cardiff began to be run down in 1962, and the last of the dinosaurs left the city's streets eight years later. By 1972, Bradford – the first and last British city to use them – had also abandoned the beautiful old beasts.

But for me, there will never be anything quite like the old trolleybuses. They are, for sure, reminders of bygone days. A low-tech world, within which these electric dinosaurs ruled the roads. Giants of their days.

It's a Great Life on the Buses

The council took a while to introduce their own fleet of motorised buses but there were private motor buses run from the early years of the century. Entrepreneur George Worrell ran the early services from his premises in Cowbridge Road East in Canton, where he had diversified from his first business venture, running a cycle shop. One route that Worrell ran, using what looks (from an old photo) like a six-seater van, was along Cathedral Road and Palace Road to Llandaff North – an early version of the 24/25 route.

Until 1954, there was no central bus station in Cardiff – only the Cardiff General train station, which was surrounded for years by a slummy area called Temperance Town. The Great Western Railway didn't particularly want their pristine and prestigious railway station to be surrounded by such a place, and they put pressure on Cardiff

Corporation, over the years, to do something about it. It was also something of an embarrassment, given its proximity to the international rugby stadium. If you see photos of the stadium from the '30s and before, the streets around it are basically a tip! (No disrespect is meant to the people who lived there, mind.)

Finally, the Corporation agreed, and in 1937 'slum clearance' began. Temperance Town was more or less demolished, leaving a clear area for development on either side (north and south) of Wood Street. This became Park Street, Havelock Square – and the Central Bus Station. The latter was not complete until after the war, though, finally opening in 1954.

In the late '50s, there were still bus terminal points all around the city centre, including St John Square, Mill Lane, Kingsway, Greyfriars Road and Windsor Lane. Not all services had to go through the Central Station, but gradually the station began to dominate and more and more services were routed through it. In the early '80s there was a further redevelopment and we ended up with more or less the bus station we have today. At the time of writing, plans are afoot for Central Square to be turned into office blocks, with the new headquarters of BBC Wales as the centrepiece. The NCP car park on the eastern side of Central Square is to be demolished and the new bus station erected in its place. Completion is due at the end of 2017, and let us hope that the people of Cardiff receive the bus station they deserve!

CITY HALL: TIMELESS GLORY

There can be few, if any, buildings that contribute to the local street scene as boldly as Cardiff's magnificent City Hall.

Approach it from the subway that runs beneath Boulevard de Nantes, and it will rise up in front of you like some majestic ocean liner: its bright, Portland stone walls shining against the sky, the fantastic clock tower that holds a four-sided clock, and a fierce and proud dragon sitting squarely on its enormous dome. The building announces, more than any other landmark in the city, 'This is Cardiff. Capital of Wales.'

Although inspired by English and French Renaissance architecture, it displays all the confidence and presence of the Edwardian era, when Cardiff's prosperity from the coal industry was at its height. Construction was completed in 1904 by local builders E. Turner & Sons, the four-year project costing £125,000 (around £13 million in today's value).

City Hall is dominated by its 194ft clock tower, whose distinctive bells first rang out on St David's Day 1905. The bells themselves are cast from tin and copper. Each features a motto. The fourth quarter bell declares, in Welsh, 'A gair Duw yn uchaf', meaning, 'God's voice on high'. The tower looks down on that famous and iconic dome, where H.C. Fehr's timeless stone dragon sits, breathing fire out across the city skyline.

Beneath the dome sits the Council Chamber, where generations of City Fathers have mapped out the city's future. The main window of the chamber is flanked by elegant stonework, which represents the rivers of Cardiff. Stone figures congregate around the facade, contemplating science, music, poetry and other burning questions to tax the soul. A magnificent scene.

If the exterior of the building is impressive, then take a moment one day to stroll inside. I have spent many hours inside City Hall, but still, as I pass beneath its stone portico, the hushed atmosphere of its interior is almost tangible. It houses grand staircases with ornate bronze balustrades, huge halls and galleries, statues of Welsh heroes installed in 1916 and, behind the scenes, a labyrinth of tiny offices, dusty storerooms and meeting rooms, where real people still work on a daily basis, delivering essential council services to the people of Cardiff.

The interior walls of the City Hall positively drip with artwork. My favourite was always E. Blair Leighton's The Shadow, *painted in 1909. The work depicts a young knight departing for battle, who poses while a fair maiden traces the profile of his shadow on to the castle wall. The strong lighting allows the maiden to capture her sweetheart's outline superbly.*

The Shadow *is one of a number of paintings that make up the Fulton Bequest, a sum bequeathed to the city in 1907 by Mrs Annie Fulton, whose husband had been Mayor of Cardiff in 1884–85. More recent pieces include a triple portrait of Diana, Princess of Wales, which became a focal point for tributes upon her death in 1997.*

Continuing the royal theme, though back outside the building, we find a fountain and pool added in front of the portico, to celebrate the investiture of Prince Charles as Prince of Wales in 1969. The fountain features jets of water arranged to replicate the three ostrich feathers of the Prince of Wales' crest. I fell in once while walking across it when it was frozen over! To the rear of the building lies Alexandra Gardens, with its impressive display of blossom-covered trees. In the centre of the gardens stands the Welsh National War Memorial, unveiled in 1928 by the Prince of Wales. Elsewhere in the park, later memorials commemorate the lives of those lost in the Falklands War in 1982.

The City Hall forms the centrepiece of a trinity of buildings that help to define this area, known generally as Cathays Park. The Law Courts, completed in 1906, sit to the west of the trio, while the National Museum of Wales, opened in 1927, completes the line-up.

The acquisition and development of the Civic Centre at Cathays Park was undoubtedly the most significant and enduring act undertaken by the former County Borough Council of Cardiff. Over the years, other buildings have been sympathetically added to this unique city-centre environment.

But without doubt, these other buildings, magnificent in their own right, pay daily homage to the sheer magnetic presence of City Hall – easily the jewel in the city's crown.

THE BEAST WITH TWO TONGUES –
CARDIFF'S COAT OF ARMS

The coat of arms of the city of Cardiff, like many other aspects of the city's culture, draws heavily on issues of ancient historic significance – as well as elements of the city's more recent past.

The current arms feature a red dragon holding a banner that shows three white chevrons on a red background. This is associated with Iestyn ap Gwrgant, the last Prince of Glamorgan, who lived in Cardiff Castle in around 1030–80. In later times, the design became the arms of the Lords of Glamorgan and Cardiff. Thus the Welsh and Norman history of the city is alluded to and the chevrons of the former arms are retained. We see the dragon planting a flagpole on a green mount, from which grows a leek, and a Tudor rose and those three ostrich feathers complete the top of the crest. The feathers form the badge of the Princes of Wales and their use was specially authorised by royal warrant. The Tudor Rose and the Mural Crown (part of the old arms of Cardiff) remind us of the city's history. The motto for the crest reads 'Deffro mae'n ddydd', which translates as 'Awake, it is day'.

The supporters are, on the right-hand side, a Welsh goat (reminiscent of the mountains of Wales) and, on the left-hand side, a hippocamp or sea horse (representing the sea and docks). The crest and the royal badge denote special royal favours to the city and the city's loyalty to the Crown.

The more modern 'logo' of the city used by the county council depicts a red dragon rising out of the waves to reach skyward. Thus it symbolises a modern city, growing from its maritime past to grasp the opportunities of the new millennium. The beast has two tongues, symbolising a commitment to both the Welsh and English languages.

*In addition to civic regalia, the traditional coat of arms
has also featured elsewhere in the city, notably on the shirts
of Cardiff Rugby Football Club and, long before the rep-
lica shirts craze, on those worn by Cardiff City in the 1927
FA Cup Final. The Lord Mayor's scouts, who escort the
civic leader at certain events, also sport the crest on their
neckerchiefs.*

Fascinating stuff, David. Now, as we are covering matters
pertaining to 'civic Cardiff', we can close this chapter with
an intriguing tale of civic disrepute, dating from 1938. Read
on to find out about …

THE DAY THE SWASTIKA
FLEW OVER CARDIFF

Of all the bizarre events to have occurred in Cardiff – such as a seal swimming up a major thoroughfare and the hosting of the *English* FA Cup finals – perhaps there is none odder than what occurred in 1938, when, for a few hours, a Nazi swastika flew over City Hall.

The infamous Nazi flag was hoisted on the City Hall flagpole next to the Union Flag to celebrate the signing of the Munich Agreement. This was the deal signed by British Prime Minister Neville Chamberlain in Munich in September 1938, with the German leader, Adolf Hitler. The deal allowed Hitler to grab a third of the territory of independent Czechoslovakia – with the Czechs allowed no real say in the matter at all.

The idea was, as Chamberlain proclaimed to the British press after landing back at RAF Northolt, to secure 'peace in our time'. After all, Hitler had given Chamberlain his solemn promise that, once Germany got their Czech land, they wouldn't try to grab anyone else's. And promises made between gentlemen are always kept, aren't they?

Now at this time, the Conservatives, led by Chamberlain, were all in favour of appeasing Hitler and keeping Britain out of any European war. Labour, though, led by Clement Attlee, had gradually come around to opposing this policy and went against the Munich deal.

So what of Cardiff and its strange flag raising? Well, apparently the Lord Mayor – one Oliver Cuthbert Purnell – took it upon himself to raise the swastika aloft. Also raised were the flags of France and Italy, which were both party to the deal, too. It seems, however, that not all of Cardiff were impressed by the sight of the swastika flying over the city. Labour councillor Allan Robinson asked why the Czech flag hadn't been flown as well, but Mayor Purnell smoothly explained that the council didn't have one.

Two other councilmen, Alderman McCale and Councillor Heginbottom, were even more aggrieved and took it upon themselves to remove the Nazi banner forthwith. Together they found their way up to the roof and pulled the thing down. Then they did something really naughty and hid it in a cupboard. But Mayor Purnell responded by simply ordering council officials to run a replacement swastika up the flag-pole. (How many of these damn swastikas did they have?!)

In fact, the Nazi flag was flown upside down and the wrong way round – as a photograph of the time reveals. It might have been inside out as well – nobody is really sure – but what *is* known for sure is that it wasn't flown properly. However, nobody down there on the streets of Cardiff really knew that at the time. To all intents and purposes, the council was celebrating Nazism.

So was Lord Mayor Purnell a Nazi sympathiser? We do not know. He did, though, offer a lengthy explanation of his actions, citing the need to retain Cardiff's position as a trading city. He stated:

> On the morning the news came through that war had been averted, I ordered the flags of the four nations to be flown. This was a gesture of goodwill to the nations concerned. It had no political or religious significance. Cardiff is a port and has to maintain friendly relationship with all nations trading with us, and it was on that ground alone that I flew the flags. Were Cardiff not a great port, the necessity would not have arisen.

The gesture does not seem to have done much to get us in Hitler's good books, though. Less than three years later, the city was blitzed by the Luftwaffe.

4

SPORTING CARDIFF

We have looked, in our previous chapters, at the historical development of Cardiff (chapters 1 and 3), and the city's cuisine (chapter 2). So, history-leisure-history – hopefully, a nice balance. We will go back to 'leisure' now, then, and have a look at some of the major sporting attractions in Cardiff.

The only problem here is, do we start with football or rugby? Well, either way was fine with me, but I had to try and remain on reasonable terms with my co-author, David Collins. So football it was!

NEVER FELT MORE LIKE SINGIN'
THE BLUES – CARDIFF CITY FC

There are lots of parks football teams in Cardiff, but professional football in the city is associated with one team, and one team only: Cardiff City Football Club (CCFC). Cardiff is not like Bristol, just across the water, which has always struggled with the problem of having two professional clubs (City and Rovers). No, in Cardiff, there has only ever been one team, and that team is 'the City'.

An interesting aspect of the City's fan base is that it stretches across not only the whole of Cardiff, but also across much of the South Wales Valleys. In this respect, CCFC is entirely different in its support from Cardiff's professional rugby team. In rugby, Valleys boys (and girls) do not support Cardiff RFC; they follow Pontypridd or one of the other Valleys clubs. In football, oddly, the Valleys folk are not merely happy to follow the City, the 'big city team', but hordes of them appear to be almost devoted to doing so. Well, you know what they say: the more the merrier ...

CCFC traces its roots back to the 1890s, when a lithographic artist from Bristol who had moved to Cardiff, Bartley Wilson, became involved with Riverside Cricket Club. Bartley was not very physically active himself, as he was disabled, walking only with the aid of crutches. But he was a formidable organiser. Once he decided that the cricketers needed something to keep them together in the winter, it did not take long for Riverside Football Club to take shape.

The club played in chocolate-and-amber quarters, a fairly unusual combination even in those days. They joined the local Cardiff and District parks league, playing home games at Sophia Gardens. The clubhouse was around the corner in Mark Street Lane in Riverside, where billiards and card games were played in the evenings, as well as air-rifle shooting.

The club was a local parks team, but Bartley watched – from his house at No. 1 Coldstream Terrace, on Canton Bridge – as, every other Saturday, hordes of spectators streamed across the bridge, coming to 'town' to watch Cardiff Rugby Club play at the Arms Park. Bartley had a dream that, a few years hence, similar hordes would come to a football ground to watch a team play the round-ball game: his team.

However, a professional team playing in a major town like Cardiff could not really be called anything as parochial as 'Riverside FC'. In 1905, when Cardiff was given city status, Bartley applied to the South Wales FA for his team to change their name to 'Cardiff City'. He was turned down, on the grounds that Riverside played in too minor a league to be entitled to such an important-sounding name.

This setback only spurred Bartley on and, within a few years, Riverside had progressed to the South Wales Amateur League, and then, in 1910, to the semi-professional Southern League (which covered the south of England, as well as South Wales). By the time the team joined the Southern League, they had already become what we know them as today: Cardiff City FC.

Joining the Southern League in 1910 was really the big step, as it meant the club becoming a professional outfit. Shares were issued and a new board of directors was formed to replace the old club committee, although Bartley was retained as the club's assistant secretary. He remained at the club, running the office, until he was in his 80s. He finally left in the mid-1950s, when he had almost come to the end of his life. He is commemorated today in the name of CCFC's official mascot, 'Bartley the Bluebird'.

The City were by this time playing in blue, and were soon to be known by their nickname: 'the Bluebirds'. This is believed to have come about after the popular play by the German writer Maurice Maeterlinck, *The Bluebird of Happiness*, came to Cardiff's New Theatre in 1913. Some punter, having seen the play, dubbed the football team 'the Bluebirds', and the name stuck. (This is why there was a 1990s Cardiff City fanzine called *O Bluebird of Happiness*. I only mention it because I was one of the two guys who started it. The other author of this book, David Collins, then started submitting pieces to the magazine as well.)

The new ground was on a council waste tip at Sloper Road, on the western fringe of the city, near Leckwith Moors. The land had been donated by the Bute family, the principal landowners in the city. The head of the family at the time was the 3rd Marquess of Bute; it was his son, Lord Ninian Crichton-Stuart, who was 'into football', and he had done most to secure the new ground for the team. The ground was therefore named 'Ninian Park'. Alas, Lord Ninian – who was also a Conservative MP for Cardiff – was to die fighting in the First World War.

The next big date in City's history came in 1920, when they were admitted into the (fully professional) Football League. City were immediately successful, winning promotion to the First Division (the top division) in their first season. For the rest of the 1920s, thousands of supporters flocked to Ninian Park every fortnight to watch the game's leading stars in action. Some of them even played for City!

This is no cheap hyperbole. In 1924, City came very close to winning the League title. On the final Saturday of the season, City needed to win at St Andrews, home of Birmingham FC (now Birmingham City). Had they won the game, they would have won the League. Alas, Len Davies' penalty for City, midway through the second half, was saved by Birmingham's England goalie Dan Tremelling, and City could only draw 0–0. News then came in 'on the wireless' that Huddersfield Town had won, and so the title went to Huddersfield.

Incidentally, Cardiff and Huddersfield finished level on points at the end of that season. Had **goal difference** been in operation, as it is now, then City would have taken the title. But **goal average** was used until 1975, and using this measurement, City missed out. It is the only time in the history of the League that the champions would have been different, had today's system been used. It is also, along with 1989, one of the two closest finishes to a League title race of all time.

In 1925, City created history again by becoming the first Welsh team to reach the final of the FA Cup. This meant a first trip to the famous Wembley Stadium. Unfortunately, City were beaten 1–0 by Sheffield United on this occasion, but two years later, City were back. In the 1927 final – the first one broadcast live on the radio – they beat Arsenal 1–0 to become the first (and only) team to 'take the trophy out of England'.

(There is a story which sometimes goes around Cardiff pubs that, because a Welsh team had won the Cup, the English FA had, henceforth, to call their competition 'the FA Cup', whereas previously it had been called 'the English Cup'. Although this story has often been repeated, sometimes in the *South Wales Echo*, I can find no reliable verification of it, and believe it is a Cardiff 'urban myth'. It is true that people in Cardiff used to call the FA Cup 'the English Cup', to distinguish it from the Welsh Cup, but it was never, as far as I can ascertain, referred to as 'the English Cup' in England. But it's a nice story …)

These years of great success were followed by ones of dismal decline. In 1929, City were relegated to the Second Division; in 1931, they went down again, to Division Three South; and they finished bottom of that league in 1934, meaning they had to apply to the other clubs to be re-elected to the League for the following season. The rest of the '30s were a grim time of lower division football and terrible attendances – partly due to the terrible economic decline, caused by the worldwide Great Depression, in the Valleys.

The post-war revival kicked off in 1947, when City ran away with the Division Three South title, setting numerous club records as they led the league virtually from start to finish. This was a team that had almost the same line-up all season – and in which ten of the starting eleven were local lads from Cardiff, Newport and the Valleys.

City were a strong side in the Second Division, and after a couple of near-misses, they returned to 'the promised land' of the First Division in 1952. The next few years were a yo-yo affair, as City were relegated in 1957, promoted again in 1960, and relegated again in 1962. Then, for the next thirteen years, there was stability, as City became almost 'hardy perennials' in the Second Division.

In the '60s and '70s, there was the added exoticism of regular European football. European competitions had been introduced by UEFA, and City seemed to be playing in Europe virtually every year – as winning the little old Welsh Cup entitled you to be in the draw for the European Cup Winners' Cup. In 1968, City almost got to the final, narrowly losing the semi-final tie to the Germans of SV Hamburg. This was after a journey of thousands of miles for the quarter-final against Dynamo Moscow, which – with Moscow frozen in the middle of winter – was played in the warmer climes of Tashkent, in the Soviet republic of Uzbekistan (now an independent country).

That was an 'away trip' which few City supporters would have made it to! However, the practice of fans going away to support the team was catching on in this era, with British Rail running 'football special' trains to coincide with matches. We also had supporters clubs sprouting up, running coaches to games.

One unfortunate consequence of the 'away trip' gaining in popularity was the growth of a new leisure-time activity called 'football hooliganism'. Some CCFC supporters, alas, became quite good at this. For quite a few years, 'the City' were better known for their fighting than their football.

City's best-ever result in Europe came in 1971, when they beat Real Madrid 1–0 at Ninian Park in a quarter-final first-leg. Alas, they went down 2–0 in Madrid in the second-leg, to go out of the competition. City never did reach that elusive European final.

Also proving elusive was the First Division. Under tough manager Jimmy Scoular (1964–73), City were often threatening to make it, but never quite doing so. A key moment, many fans of that era believed, came in October 1970, when star centre forward John Toshack was sold to Liverpool for a club record fee, at a time when City were top of the

Second Division. 'Tosh' became a star at Anfield, winning trophies galore, but City finished third and missed out on promotion by 4 points. It was to prove their last real chance to get back to 'the top flight' for some thirty-five years.

The next quarter-century were years of grim decline, as bad as the cruel 1930s – and lasting for far longer. Attendances shrank once more as hooliganism took its toll and, on the pitch, performances went from bad to worse. In 1975, City ended a run of almost thirty years in the top two divisions, by going down to the Third. After a few years of yo-yoing, they went down to the almost unthinkable depths of the Fourth Division in 1986.

There were more hapless years of yo-yoing, this time between the Third and Fourth, with four relegations and four promotions (and the birth of The Ayatollah!), before City finally put the Fourth behind them for good (we hope!) in 2001. Two years later, they returned to a place they had not been in for eighteen years, the 'Second Division' – now known as the Championship.

So could City now reach the Premier League? Well, there were some years of stumbling and bumbling, with City having a few promotion near-misses under manager Dave Jones (2005–11), who seemed to be the modern equivalent of Jimmy Scoular. So near and yet so far!

There were also more trips to Wembley – loads of them! Having not been to the famous stadium since 1927, City were finally there again in 2008, for an FA Cup semi-final (against Barnsley); and again, a few weeks later, for the Cup final (against Portsmouth); and again, in 2010, for a play-off final (against Blackpool); and again, in 2012, for a Carling Cup final (against Liverpool). Liverpool fans in the '80s took to calling the place 'Anfield South'. City fans in recent years might have been forgiven for calling it 'Ninian East'!

Oh, that reminds me: another funny thing happened along the way. After ninety-nine years, in 2009, we didn't play at Ninian Park anymore. That summer, the bulldozers moved in to demolish lovely old Ninian (for a housing estate), and City moved in 'across the road' (Sloper Road, that is) at the swanky new ground, very inventively named 'the Cardiff City Stadium'.

Premier League football finally arrived in 2013, courtesy of promotion under new boss Malky Mackay. City made a big impact by winning their first home game against the eventual champions, Manchester City. But this was one of a mere handful of victories all season, as City went straight back down, with barely a whimper, in bottom place.

So now the side embark on another campaign in the Championship. Owner Vincent Tan, a multimillionaire (some say billionaire) Malaysian businessman, has spent a lot of money and will be banking on promotion back to the big-money league, the Premier. There will be a lot of pressure on the team and their current manager, former Man Utd 'super-sub' striker Ole Gunnar Solskjaer, to deliver. (Oops! Since writing this, Ole has gone. The City boss is now Russell Slade.)

Of course, Mr Tan has been in the news rather a lot since he took over the club in 2011 – and when I say the news, I mean the national news, not the *South Wales Echo*. His 'rebranding' of the club, from the traditional blue shirts to red ones (because red is a lucky colour in Asia), has proven to be a very divisive issue among Cardiff fans. Mercifully, common sense later prevailed.

I will not dwell any longer on the 'red/blue' issue. Let us just hope that soon City can make the news for what they do on the pitch, rather than off it! Knowing 'the City', though, that is some hope.

Okay, that's the football. On to the rugby …

CHASING THE EGG – RUGBY IN CARDIFF

Now, my co-author, David Collins, doesn't really 'do' rugby. And I am a long-standing season ticket holder at Cardiff City – the football team, right? – so I shouldn't really be saying this. But I am going to anyway …

Rugby is part of the very essence of Cardiff.

I knew this growing up in Pontcanna, a mere mile upstream and downwind of the rugby stadium. On international days, you could hear the 'roar' when Wales scored. I heard these roars when I was outside the house, playing in the street, in the days when I was too young to even comprehend what rugby was.

Later, once I got interested in the game, you could hear the roars on the TV as well. Wales games were a big deal in the 1970s. You have to remember, Wales did not lose at home in the Five Nations from 1969 until 1982 – that was twenty-seven games without defeat. The new National Stadium (opened in 1970), with its 'wall of sound' effect, was widely believed to be utterly impregnable. Or almost. Only New Zealand could beat Wales there, which they did in 1972 and again in 1978 – although on the latter occasion there were strong allegations of cheating.

Many times, Wales were behind going into the final quarter of the game, only for Gareth Edwards, or Barry John (or, later, Phil Bennett), or Gerald Davies, or – if it was against England – J.P.R. Williams to pull off some miraculous move and spark a decisive score.

As a kid, this was all gripping stuff. My older brother had schooled me in the mechanics of watching Wales, by forcing me to learn, and then repeat, the names of all the players. I can still reel off the 1976 Grand Slam side (learned at the age of 7!) to this day.

Some of it was a bit tricky, though; 'Quinnell' and 'Gravell' both played for Llanelli, both had weird names and both sported fearsome-looking beards – Quinnell, I suppose, looked more like a Viking warrior and Gravell a zestful Welsh bard. Both Williamses (J.P.R. and J.J.) had initials instead of names (because, I later discovered, **they both had the same name:** John Williams) and both of them had side-burns. But I soon learned that J.P.R. was the one who played like an utter, utter maniac (in a good way). He seemed to smash that French winger, Gourdon, into the seventh row of the seats. And this guy is a doctor! There were also the two Davieses, Gerald and Mervyn, who both had moustaches. But Gerald was the guy who swerved around all the defenders, and Merve – confusingly nicknamed 'Merve the Swerve' – was the towering headband at the back of the line-out.

It was all gripping stuff, as I say, watching these demonic warriors (the forwards, plus J.P.R.) and twinkled-toed genies (the backs – the peerless, unforgettable Edwards in particular). But there was something a bit ... inevitable ... about it all. Wales always won.

Remember, all this began for me in 1976, when Wales won the Grand Slam. After they beat Ireland in the opening game of '77, I was fairly complacent about their abilities. My brother was even more so.

Just before they kicked off in Paris in '77, my next-door neighbour, Martin Conde, called at the house. He wanted to play, outside. Wales are about to kick-off, and he wanted to play. I turned to my brother. 'Nick, are Wales gonna win this game?'

He gave me a stern look. 'Don't be so stupid. Of course they're gonna win.'

Thus assured, I went outside to play. I came back a couple of hours later, exhausted by the rigours of rat-a-tat ginger. My brother looked even sterner than before. 'Nick,' I asked him, still complacent, 'did Wales win, then?'

Now he gave me a dirty look. 'No, they bloody didn't,' he said, and stormed out of the room. In an instant, my world fell in. This was the first time I realised that Wales could lose at rugby.

By the mid-1980s, Wales seemed to be losing all the time. Occasionally I went to Cardiff rugby games and, if I had been part of a circle of mates going there, I might have become a regular at the Arms Park. Instead, a few of us started going 'down the City', and that habit instantly stuck. I made occasional forays to the rugby, if City were away or not playing, but by now I was aware of 'the culture gap' between rugby and football in Cardiff. Everyone down the City seemed to detest rugby, and called its supporters 'rugger buggers'. The game itself was derisively referred to as 'chasing the egg'. So I kind of sneaked down the Arms Park every now and then, because I knew that what I was doing, in strict ideological terms, was 'not quite right'.

Now, this antipathy between football and rugby hasn't always existed, as far as I can tell. Many sports fans of an older generation talk of days like the one in 1961, when Wales played England at the Arms Park in the afternoon, after which thousands of supporters trooped down Tudor Street to Ninian Park, where City – then in the First Division – were taking on mighty Spurs, who were going for the League and Cup double. City won 3–2, one of a mere handful of defeats for Spurs in their momentous year.

So football and rugby *did* mix, to some extent, back then. For some people, they still do. For myself, I prefer, like many unaffiliated South Walians (those who do not go to watch a particular club), to 'mix and match' the two games. I only pay to see Cardiff City, but I will watch club games and Wales games on the telly. I won't pretend I'm not interested!

To me, the true nature of 'bi-culturalism' in Cardiff is not speaking both English and Welsh (few, in percentage terms, actually do), but being interested in both football and rugby. And, although fans of Gareth Bale and Aaron Ramsey will not want to hear this, I will say it anyway: Gareth Edwards is the closest thing to a genius I have seen in any sporting arena. (Diego Maradona is second.)

Now, on one point I will agree with the anti-rugby crowd, to an extent: the Wales rugby experience, at the stadium itself, is now a bit naff. In the '70s, in a largely male environment, the crowd would sport witty banners like 'Gravell Eats Soft Centres', 'Pricey Brings 'Em Down to Earth' (Graham Price being the formidable scrummaging Welsh prop) and 'Inter-City Elgan 125' (Elgan Rees being the speedy winger). There would be a brass band and the singing would be done by the crowd rather than by professional singers 'leading the crowd'.

Anyway, so far I have attempted to tackle (geddit?) the subject of rugby, without yet mentioning the thing that kicked off the game in the city, which was Cardiff RFC. Cardiff, the 'Blue-and-Blacks', predates the city's football club by some years, tracing its origins to a founding meeting in 1876. Originally, the team's kit was a black-and-white skull-and-crossbones affair. This, though, was deemed to be a tad morbid and was soon changed to the blue-and-black colours of Cambridge University after one of the Cardiff players, who was at college at Cambridge, brought a Cambridge strip to the Cardiff dressing room one Saturday.

By the turn of the century, Cardiff RFC was a well-established attraction, drawing big crowds to their ground in the centre of 'town'. Cardiff Arms Park also hosted Welsh rugby internationals. The Cardiff club itself played host to major touring sides, like the All Blacks (New Zealand) and the Springboks (South Africa), and regularly provided a number of players not only to Wales, but also to the British Isles touring sides (later called the British Lions). They also

had a major part to play in the development of rugby forma-
tions, with centre Frank Hancock (of the Hancocks brewing
family) inspiring a move, in 1883, from nine forwards and
six backs, to eight-and-seven; within a couple of years, this
new formation had been universally adopted throughout
the world of rugby. It has been used ever since.

Cardiff RFC was a famous side after the Second World
War, when they regularly attracted gates in the 40,000s,
much like Cardiff City Football Club did in the same era.
At this point they really were one of the most prestigious
clubs in the whole of Britain. Welshmen from throughout
the Principality, as well as well-known international players,
came to Cardiff to don the famous blue-and-black jersey.
Cardiff was frequently top of the 'Welsh merit table', which
was a kind of league based on win percentages. There was
no official league, because every rugby club had its own fixture list; all games were technically friendlies, and no two
clubs played exactly the same teams. In this way, amateur
rugby union was completely different to professional football, which operated on a strict league system.

The really big fixtures in Cardiff's list in those days were
against the touring sides – like New Zealand, whom Cardiff
famously beat in 1953 – and against their local rivals,
Newport (affectionately known as 'the black-and-amber
bastards'). Cardiff and Newport would clash four times every
season: twice at home and twice away. The big deal was to
win the lot, but nobody – not Cardiff, not Newport – ever
quite managed it. Eventually, by the 1970s, some kind of
sanity had overtaken this intense parochialism, and Newport
and Cardiff were only colliding twice every season.

There was a lot of pressure on the fixture secretary at Cardiff,
because so many teams wanted to play them – many of them
in England. At one point in the post-war years, such was the
pressure that Cardiff took the decision to play two teams every

week, one at home and one away. There was no distinction between the two, there were just two 'Cardiff' first teams! This experiment did not last long, though. Instead, we had the first team and the Athletic, who were effectively the 'seconds' and who played their home games for years at Sophia Gardens, next to the cricket ground. Some fairly good players preferred to turn out for the Athletic, rather than join a 'first-class' team like Pontypridd or Ebbw Vale, because they had such an affection for the club. (In the 1970s and '80s, names like Terry Charles, Steve Blackmore and Tim Crothers come to mind.)

Now, like everything else in Cardiff, it has all changed – several times in the case of Cardiff rugby. In the mid-'80s, the leagues were introduced, despite a lot of opposition, meaning that clubs were no longer in charge of their own fixture lists. In the mid-'90s, this was followed by professionalism, meaning that top clubs now needed to pay their players to attract the best ones and compete with their rivals. Finally, in 2003, we got regional rugby, which meant that there were now only four (initially five) fully professional teams – called 'regions' – in Wales.

Cardiff was deemed important enough, as a rugby centre, to have its own region, and Cardiff RFC owner Peter Thomas – a man of considerable wealth due to the success of the family firm 'Peter Pies', which had been sold off for a large amount – became the boss of Cardiff Blues. (I should also mention that Peter 'the Pieman' also played for the club for several seasons during the 1950s.) Cardiff RFC, meanwhile, has continued as a club in the Welsh Premiership and is now a feeder club to the Blues.

For most fans, the Blues – who play in essentially the same colours as Cardiff RFC – is now basically what 'Cardiff RFC' used to be: the city's big rugby club. There was a flirtation with playing at the football ground, the Cardiff City Stadium (which the rugby boys derisively dubbed 'Legoland'!), but they are now back in their heartland at the Arms Park, which most fans regard as their 'birthright'.

The Arms Park is a unique venue, in that it is so close to the pubs of the city centre. Certainly the Blues fans did not want to be ferried out to Leckwith by shuttle bus every fortnight. The ground, too, has less than half the capacity of the football ground, so it is far easier to generate the required 'atmosphere' there. It has its attractive quirks, too, like the balconies of the apartments on Westgate Street, from where in past years supporters – and merely curious residents – have watched games. The 'balconies' thing was a feature of national TV in the '70s, whenever Cardiff games were featured on BBC2's *Rugby Special* on Sunday. There was really no other ground in Britain quite like it.

It is great for the club's supporters that the Blues moved back to the Arms Park. The problem is, there are not enough of them anymore. Regional rugby has its drawbacks for the potential fan, in that it never kicks off in the traditional Saturday afternoon slot anymore; and, as there are now only four Welsh teams for the TV boys to choose from and two live games a week, nearly all of the home games end up being televised anyway – so there is no particular

need to attend. To add to the club's woes, more and more of the younger generation – who might, in years gone by, have been taken to Cardiff rugby games by beaming parents – are now being raised as Cardiff City football fans.

So the future for Cardiff Blues is uncertain. What is very certain, though, is that there is still a thriving club rugby scene within the city, with a host of clubs having active senior and youth sections: teams like Canton, Llandaff and Glamorgan Wanderers (for years, a first-class club themselves) in the west of the city; Llandaff North, Whitchurch, Rhiwbina and Llanishen in the north; St Peters, St Albans and Rumney to the east, to name but a few. South Cardiff has always had its famous multi-ethnic CIACS (*kye-aks*). It is this local 'heartbeat' that ensures the game keeps going, whatever the politicking at the top.

For me, one of the great things about Cardiff, as a rugby city, is its localism. In what other city could you wander into a city-centre bar (the Borough, say) and find one of the game's all-time international greats, Barry John, sitting with a pint of beer and a newspaper in front of him, 'doing the horses'? Or be sat in a local in Canton (the Romilly) when another one – Jonathan Davies, the original Jonathan Davies, that is – wanders in and asks if he can join in a game of darts with you? Nowhere, that's where!

The Butchers Arms in Llandaff is a veritable goldmine of former stars of the game. For years, the famous Welsh centre pairing of the '50s, Bleddyn Williams and Dr Jack Matthews (another mad doctor!), would sit there together, still great mates. John Dawes, a British Lions captain and coach, can sometimes be seen there. And many others besides.

I was aware of this local aspect from an early age. I chatted to Gerald Davies when I was about 8, when he was lounging about in my local swimming pool (the National Sports Centre). I knew him, see, because he had presented the prizes at the Llandaff RFC annual 'do'. And he was down-to-earth enough to act as though he knew *me*. My oldest sister Joanna was in the same class at Bishop Hannan High School as Terry Holmes, the 'battering ram' Wales scrum-half, and, at the time, she was taller than him!

Now these guys are famous players, even in international circles. Yes, I have seen Graham Kavanagh from the City having a pint with Andy Campbell at Mulligans bar, and Phil Dwyer (a genuine City legend, mind) is always propping up the bar at Canton Wetherspoons, but it is not really the same, is it?

DIAMOND GEEZERS – BASEBALL

Now this bit may reveal what sort of reader you are.

If you are a visitor to our fair city – or maybe have never even been – you will find this entry somewhat bizarre. A real 'well, I never knew that' moment.

*On the other hand, if you are a native Cardiffian, you would be amazed if a book such as this **didn't** feature an account of this popular city pastime.*

For the game of baseball is – like many other products, places and people featured in these pages – a part of life here. The game tends to be known as 'Welsh Baseball' – though north of the M4 it remains a mystery. Anything much further west than Culverhouse Cross and it is unheard of. Newport 'do' it, but only just. Life 'on the diamond' is proper Cardiff, see.

The sport we now know as Welsh (or, more accurately, British) baseball dates back to 1892. At that time, the English and Welsh governing bodies changed the name from 'rounders' to better reflect the speed of the game. Although contests between teams from different areas took place, proper rules didn't emerge until the twentieth century. The first international game between Wales and England

*took place in Cardiff, at the Harlequins Playing Fields –
now home of St Peters RFC – in 1908.*

*Unified rules were formalised in 1927 (a key year in the
sporting history of the city!) with the formation of the
International Baseball Board (which remains the sport's governing body), and representatives from the Welsh Baseball
Union and the Liverpool-based English Baseball Association.*

*Today, the game remains in Britain only in its heartlands
of Cardiff, a bit of Newport and, bizarrely, Liverpool.
Whilst there may not be the eight or so divisions that
existed in the 1980s, the passion remains for those – players,
coaches, organisers, supporters – at the heart of the game.*

*There are similarities with the American version of the
game, of course. Yeah, a bloke chucks a ball at another
guy, who whacks it away with a stick, before attempting
to run around a diamond while a load of other guys try to
find the thing. But culturally, the games are worlds apart.
We wear proper kit, like a football team, rather than pyja-
mas. We don't wear caps, either. US baseball is played in
vast arenas where the whole family enjoys a day out. Welsh
baseball is played on the muddy fields of Cardiff parks. And
they don't sell popcorn at Splott Park, believe me.*

*It is hard to overstate the place of baseball in Cardiff cul-
ture. To this day, it remains one of the few sports that I was
actually taught in school. I mean properly **taught**. Where to
stand, how to run, how to turn right if you were stopping
at base 3 … We even had a selection of different-sized bats
to choose from, before stepping up to the pegs to face the
demon bowler, who would hurl the rock-hard ball at you,
underarm but **ferociously**, in an attempt to either deceive or
maim you. And this was junior school, by the way. We are
probably talking about 8 year olds here.*

*Perhaps the appeal of the game lies in the fact that, well,
anyone can enjoy it. The most athletic kids in the class can*

whack the ball with gusto, while the skinny, rubbish ones (like me) don't even have to hit it to make a run. As long as you swing the bat in the general direction of the ball, that's good enough to let you try and make a run. Footballers and rugby players use the game to keep fit in the summer close season. Famous baseballers who became notable in other sports include John Toshack, Terry Yorath, Nathan Blake and Phil Dwyer (football), Terry Holmes, Mark Ring and David Bishop (rugby union), and even Wigan Rugby League legend Jim Sullivan.

Baseball tends to be a working-class game in Cardiff. The names of local sides read like a road map of the old industrial city. There are Splott Cons, Rumney RFC, the afore-mentioned St Peters (from Roath) and, of course, Grange Albion – 'Grange' referring to Grangetown. Then there are names which are no more – names of clubs like Llanrumney Youth, St Pats and Splott US. Names of old players like Bill Barrett (later a widely read city historian), Paddy Hennessy, Anki Saunders and Ted Peterson, whose achievements in the game led to him being awarded an MBE. The game truly enjoys a rich history, in which the famous black-and-gold of St Albans and the almost sacred black-and-white stripes of Grange Albion form just a part of the tapestry.

Indeed, Grange Albion represent a fascinating case study of the history of the game. One of the oldest surviv-ing clubs (formed in 1907), they are the only one to have played in every single season of the Welsh Baseball League. They are the most successful club in Welsh baseball, having been Dewar Shield Champions a record thirty-four times. They have also supplied the Welsh international team with more players than any other club.

But don't be thinking that these guys have their heads stuck in the past. These days, the club boasts a lively and informa-tive website, has corporate sponsors and runs a women's section. Across the city, the game is played by both boys and girls and men and women – in fact, the ladies league now have more teams than the men's and is positively thriving.

Baseball's peak came after the wars: in 1924, there were 10,000 people watching the Wales v England international at the Arms Park. In 1948, the record crowd of 16,000 watched the same fixture. Even important club games could attract crowds of thousands in those eras.

Yes, truly baseball is a game for everyone. Pot-bellied dads can run around Sevenoaks Park in Grangetown for fifteen weeks each summer, while the arithmetic complications brought about by two teams batting twice, along with extras, byes and 'two goods and out', will keep the most meticulous of scorers busy for hours.

Finally, it is a team game, within which individuals of all ability can flourish or fail. A metaphor for life itself!

Newsflash: in August 2014, demon Grange Albion bowler Matthew Hopkins bowled the England team out for 1 run, breaking a fifty-year-old record held by Paddy Hennessy.

Wow! Baseball, eh? Well, it may indeed be 'a Cardiff thing', but growing up in Pontcanna, I have to say I was barely aware of the game – although there are diamonds in the summer over Llandaff Fields. Is it actually a 'parts of Cardiff thing'? Anyway, we now have a piece on 'baseball for poshos'!

FOREVER BATTING ON A STICKY WICKET – ADVENTURES OF GLAMORGAN COUNTY CRICKET CLUB

When I was 10 years old, I began to read sports reports in the newspapers – principally the *Daily Mail*, as that was the paper my mother bought (for the crossword). Although

I initially picked up her discarded paper to read the football reports, I soon became aware of – and vaguely interested in – the other stuff.

The summer dawned, and with it the 1979 cricket season. I already knew about the England team and 'Test' matches, because they were on TV all the time. (Why were they called that, though? What were they testing?)

I then became aware that there was this other thing called county cricket, and that Cardiff's team was 'Glamorgan'. The third thing I became aware of was that this Glamorgan outfit, captained by Robin Hobbs, were bottom of the seventeen-team county championship. It wasn't a strong position, really, from which to try to convince a 10-year-old kid to follow his local cricket team.

Glamorgan were generally quite poor over the next couple of years, and it became settled in my mind that they were, always had been and always would be one of the weakest teams in the Championship. Perhaps they were lucky even to be *in* the damn Championship, as there were plenty of counties that weren't – Devon, Dorset, Wiltshire, Berkshire, Durham – maybe some of which would have been better than us, given the chance.

The only thing that really fascinated me about Glamorgan was that they were *local*. I could walk the dog over Pontcanna Fields, take a turning along the path by the River Taff and then – from the raised bank – peer between the stands and into the cricket ground. I would stand there, fascinated, for what seemed like hours at a time – sometimes even when there was a game going on.

Somerset were a big attraction back then, in the early '80s. They had Ian Botham, the cavalier England all-rounder, as well as the two swaggering West Indians, Viv Richards (master batsman) and Joel Garner (fearsome opening bowler). There was a gap between two of the stands, and there was a place on the bank where you could stand so that you were right in line with the batsman's line of vision as the bowler charged up to him from the Cathedral Road End. I remember standing there as 'Big Bird' Garner came rampaging up the field, all 7ft 10in of him, or whatever he was – it was a daunting sight. John Hopkins, our opening bat, must have been shaking like a leaf!

On summer evenings, chaps with ties and briefcases would gather at this point, on their way home from work, to espy the latest developments at the crease. Sometimes it seemed like there were more of us stood there on that damn bank than there were inside the ground. No wonder Glamorgan always had financial problems!

I can't remember who most of the players were, because the only one who ever seemed to do anything was a South African all-rounder called Rodney Ontong. You would open the paper and who had taken 5 for 66 to prevent an innings defeat? Rodney Ontong. The following week at Canterbury, who hit a battling 73 not out to avoid the follow-on? Ontong, of course. I wondered why they didn't just call them 'Rodneyontongshire'.

At some point, some kind of historical consciousness began to creep into my brain. Somebody – probably my father – randomly mentioned one day that Glamorgan had actually **won** the County Championship, not once, but twice. In 1948 and 1969 to be precise. This blew my mind. I could imagine nothing more far-fetched than the idea that Glamorgan had ever won anything.

But it was true. Glamorgan, in fact, had a rich history – although not a lot happened for a few years after they joined the County Championship in 1921. Then came 1948. The '48 side was captained by an extraordinary character named Wilf Wooller. Wilf was a famous rugby centre before the war, who became a famous cricketer after it. He had played for Wales at rugby while he was still a schoolboy (albeit a slightly over-age one) in his native North Wales, and had played in the 1935 Wales team that beat the All Blacks.

Wilf Wooller was one of the great sporting all-round-ers. After graduating from Cambridge, he came to work in Cardiff and, naturally, joined the city's famous rugby club. In the summer, he played cricket for local village side St Fagans (more on them later), and in the winter, he played rugby for Cardiff and Wales. Except that he also turned out (at centre forward) for one of Cardiff City's reserve sides – at football, that is. Although City did not sign him up (or, perhaps, he did not want to lose his amateur status), Wilf still experimented with the notion of turning out for

Barry Town (football) in midweek and playing for Cardiff at rugby on the weekend. I don't think you had to spend any time training in those days, mind.

To add to the sporting madness, Wilf played for Cardiff Athletic club at bowls and won international caps for Wales at squash. (There was another bloke like this in Cardiff after the war, who played everything. He had played rugby for Ireland: his name was Des O'Brien.)

Anyway, back to the cricket. Wilf survived Changi jail – the Japanese prisoner-of-war camp in Singapore – and after the war he focused on his all-round skills as a batsman and bowler in the white-flannel game. Having moved up from St Fagans to Glamorgan in the late '30s, he now took over as county captain – and secretary. (There was a lot of multi-tasking in those days.)

In 1948, Wilf ended thirty years of, essentially, non-achievement for Glamorgan by skippering them to the county title. Although Wilf had spread his talents around several sports, he now realised the importance of proper preparation for games. His Glamorgan players were particularly noted for their fielding ability, a prowess that was honed only after long practice sessions in the nets. Team bonding was then developed by long 'practice' sessions in the bar afterwards!

Wilf was twice picked for England tours overseas – or, rather, MCC tours, as they were known in those days. (England played in home Test matches; overseas tours were conducted not by 'England', but by 'the MCC'.) Unfortunately, business commitments meant that he could not make either the 1948–49 or 1951–52 trips.

Yes, Wilf Wooller, one of Cardiff's truly remarkable characters! While Wilf was unquestionably the bulwark of the 1948 side, the next triumphant Glamorgan team – in 1969, twenty-one years later – had many stars. The skipper was the dashing Tony Lewis, a middle-order bat who became, in 1972, the last man to captain England on his Test debut. He is also the only Glamorgan player ever to skipper England and went on to be the BBC's main cricket presenter for some years. Tony Lewis apart, there was the all-rounder Peter Walker (middle-order bat and left-arm spinner – although he batted right-handed), who was later the chief sports reporter on BBC Wales' *Wales Today*. There was exotic foreign talent, too, in the shape of the Pakistani master batsman Majid Khan, and there was bowling fire from Jeff Jones, regarded as the fastest bowler in the country at that time. Walker and Jones also won Test caps for England.

I should also mention Malcolm Nash. He is normally remembered as the guy who was hit for the first-ever 'six sixes in an over' by Gary Sobers in a Glamorgan *v* Notts game at St Helen's, Swansea, in 1968. However, this misfortune occurred at a time when Malcolm was experimenting with spin bowling. He quickly reverted to his former seam-bowling style and in the Championship-winning season, he was Glamorgan's leading wicket-taker, with seventy-one victims – as well as contributing a handy batting average of 22. An unsung hero indeed.

So, Glamorgan had once been good. In the '90s, they amazed me by becoming good again. The Sunday League was secured on a balmy afternoon at Canterbury in 1993; the third and final (to date!) County Championship followed four years later, in 1997. This was the Glamorgan of reliable opener Hugh Morris, dashing middle-order bat Matthew Maynard, charismatic spinner Robert Croft and pacey strike bowler Steve Watkin.

Times have been decidedly lean on the pitch since the likes of Croft retired. Much money was spent on the stadium, which has now hosted England one-day internationals and Test games (beginning with the nail-biting Ashes Test in 2009). This has generated revenue for the club, but of course there was a big cost in building it, and Glamorgan supporters have yet to see any real benefits in improved performances on the field. They are currently in the lower tier of both the County Championship and the Sunday League.

But whatever happens, Glamorgan are unique. For a start, they are the only Welsh county playing in the County Championship. 'Croftie' has stated that 'playing for Glamorgan was like playing for Wales. Playing for England was like playing for the British Lions.'

(A quick note here: in Test cricket, 'England' is actually short for 'England and Wales' – this is the honest truth, although nobody in England ever believes me – so Welsh players can play for 'England'. That is why England can also play Tests in Wales.)

For seventy years, Glamorgan was the newest of the seventeen teams in the County Championship. Durham messed that up when they were admitted in 1991. But Glamorgan still hold two other records. For one thing, they are the only one of the eighteen teams never to have won a one-day final at Lords, having lost there in finals in 1977, 2000 and 2013.

And for the other, they have regularly, in past years, staged home games outside the county of Glamorgan, at places like Abergavenny (Monmouthshire), Colwyn Bay (Denbighshire in North Wales) and Cresselly (in Pembrokeshire, in the far west) – backing up Croftie's assertion that, in many ways, 'Glamorgan', in cricket terms, is really 'Wales'.

Just a quick mention of club cricket before we leave the subject entirely. One of the useful feeder clubs for Glamorgan has been St Fagans, situated in a former village (now another suburb of Cardiff) to the west of the city, near the banks of the River Ely. St Fagans reached the Village Cup final a couple of years running in the early '80s and have provided a testing ground for many future Glamorgan stars, Wilf Wooller and Matthew Maynard among them.

St Fagans provides a serene setting for village cricket, and if you have a yen for this kind of thing, it is worth checking their fixture list.

THE DAY DR JACK FOUGHT ROCKY

In the 1950s, Jack Matthews was a rock-hard centre for Cardiff and Wales, who also practised as a doctor. On the rugby pitch, he seemed to specialise in smashing opponents to bits; off it, he put them together again.

In 1943, Jack went to RAF St Athan with the Cardiff Medics boxing team, to fight against a side assembled from the US Army platoon who were stationed there. He came up against Rocky Marciano – later the undefeated heavyweight champion of the world.

The fight was a four-round contest. Marciano had stopped his previous six opponents but Dr Jack was no shrinking violet. The bout finished in a draw. Dr Jack gained many free pints over the years from telling this story. And the amazing thing is, it was true.

5

AROUND
THE DISTRICTS

Back to the story of Cardiff ...

Eventually, as the city expanded, it became a fairly sprawling place of many different districts. There are far too many of them to even think of covering them all in one book, so here we will look at just a few. Apologies if your own district is 'missed out'. Maybe we will cover it in Volume II ...

BUTETOWN:
THEY USED TO CALL IT TIGER BAY ...

These days we are asked to say 'Cardiff Bay', but to older generations of Cardiffians the area now inhabited by swanky cafe bars and trendy apartments will forever be known by other, longer-established names: 'Butetown', 'the Docks' or even the almost archaic term, 'Tiger Bay'.

The origins of this last, colourful monicker are hard to establish. It has been suggested by some that it is attributable to the ferocious currents around the local tidal stretches, where the River Severn meets the Bristol Channel. The fast-moving waters are said to have reminded sailors of the rapid movement of tigers. This may or may not be true, but what cannot be questioned is that the name came to describe an eclectic melting pot of multiracial life, which played as much of a part in the development of the city as the construction of the docks themselves.

Tiger Bay had over fifty nationalities living there at one time. Some of the largest communities included the Somalis, the Yemenis and the Greeks. There were also plenty of Scandinavians – hence the Norwegian church. Residents of many races and backgrounds socialised together and inter-married, creating a distinct community among the 10,000 people living in this patch.

Tiger Bay has produced its share of celebrities. Among them are Joe Erskine, the boxer who became British heavy-weight champion; Billy Boston, a legendary try-scoring winger in rugby league; Paulo Radmilovic, a water polo player and swimmer, who won gold medals at the 1908, 1912 and 1920 Olympic Games; and Betty Campbell, the first black headmistress in Wales.

It is worth pausing on Mrs Campbell. She was head teacher for twenty-eight years at Mount Stuart School. In later years she represented the Butetown ward on the city council. She remembered how, as a young girl, she didn't have to learn about other countries and cultures from a book because, in Butetown, 'it was all here for us in real life'. When it was Easter time, she went to the Greek church. When it was Mohammedan Festival, the locals dressed in a headscarf and everyone was made welcome with apples and oranges. So, she explains, people learned about different religions just by meeting people who had a different religion.

The name Tiger Bay itself has been captured in song. Check out the lyrics of 'Hit Me With Your Rhythm Stick', the 1978 chart-topper from Ian Dury: 'In the dock of Tiger Bay / On the road to Mandalay / From Bombay to Santa Fe / Over hills and far away.' Later, St Etienne recorded an album, which they called Tiger Bay.

The word 'Butetown', however, seems to have been air-brushed out of history.

The best-selling novelist Alexander Cordell also had much affection for this intriguing patch of old Cardiff. Although usually associated with historical tales of life in the South Wales Valleys during the Industrial Revolution, Cordell's Tales from Tiger Bay, *published in 1986, is well worth a read. The book features thirteen short stories linked to the adventures of Cardiff's own Jim Driscoll, 'Peerless Jim'. These tales, which are crammed with the sights, sounds and colours of Cardiff, are narrated by the different people themselves, and provide a colourful insight into their ways of life.*

Cardiff's docks were, at the time of the First World War, the busiest in Britain, and indeed the world. The cosmopolitan community of Tiger Bay was also one of the most well known in Britain. Eventually, this community played a central role in a major cinema film.

The 1959 film *Tiger Bay*, starring John Mills, included many scenes shot in the docks area. The film describes the tale of a 12-year-old tomboy (John Mills' daughter Hayley Mills, in her first film), who witnesses the murder of a woman (Yvonne Mitchell) by her Polish sailor boyfriend Korchinsky (Horst Buchholz). The police superintendent (John Mills) is anxious to arrest Korchinsky, but the girl forms a bond with him and tries to protect him from the police. There is a rousing climax as the police race along the coast road, trying to intercept the boat that Korchinsky is on, which is sailing down the Bristol Channel. They have to stop him before the boat gets 12 miles out to sea, or he will be in international waters and beyond their custody.

Although this is a reasonable watch, and is especially interesting for Cardiffians, there are several confusing geographical aspects. For instance, the film-makers (Independent Artists and the Rank Organisation) decided that alongside scenes of street life in Cardiff Docks, they would include the iconic Transporter Bridge – except that that is in Newport Docks, 12 miles away! Never mind, they stuck it in, anyway. I have often wondered how many people visited Cardiff Docks as a result of seeing this film, and wondered where the famous Transporter Bridge was.

Back to the film. On a Saturday night, following the murder, Korchinsky walks away from the docklands streets to evade the police, taking the girl with him. In the next scene, they wake up the following morning in an abandoned monastery on a rural hillside, with sheep roaming around! It is as though the film-makers thought that you only had to walk ten minutes from the docks before you were up in the hills!

Finally, the chase to intercept the ship at the end. We see endless shots of John Mills, in his police car, hurtling along a coast road. This is the road to Swanbridge and Sully Island (St Mary's Well Bay Road), which culminates in a dead end at the beach. However, although we knew that, people in the rest of Britain didn't, and I suppose the way it is edited looks quite exciting.

Hayley Mills went on to become a big teenage star, and made six films for Disney. Horst Buchholz was one of *The Magnificent Seven* the following year. But Newport Transporter Bridge never transferred to Cardiff …

Tiger Bay was notorious. Although there was general harmony between all the different races, the area had a well-earned reputation as a hotbed of immorality. It was rife with prostitution, gambling and violence, and was considered to be a very rough and dangerous area. Merchant ships arrived

*from all over the globe, loaded with rough and rowdy
seamen, who only stayed long enough to unload and reload
their ships.*

*Tiger Bay offered all the comforts that the sailors
demanded, and so prevalent was its reputation for vice and
immorality that the name 'Tiger Bay' became a general term,
to be applied to any dock or seaside neighbourhood with a
similar notoriety for crime and violence.*

*The mighty Bute Street, the very spine of Tiger Bay, was
once home to thirty pubs, from the notorious Custom
House, to the Cape Horn and the Barley Mow – with the
Glastonbury, the Fishguard and the Salutation nearer town.
On Crichton Street, running off Bute Street, the Quebec
attracted people from all over the city, who were there to
sing-along with guitar-strumming Vic Parker, an unforgettable Cardiff legend. Vic was honoured with a traditional
Tiger Bay funeral, mourners swaying and dancing behind a
jazz band that could have come direct from New Orleans!*

Although the docks went into decline from the end of the
First World War onwards, the cultural 'after-life' of the
industry – the pubs and hideaway drinking dens called 'shebeens' – continued to draw generations of Cardiffians who
were not from the area 'down the Docks', particularly on
Saturday nights. Each generation had a different favourite nightspot. In the '80s, one of the popular ones was the
Casablanca Club, where you could always get something a
little bit more exotic than tobacco to smoke.

The 1960s saw the wholesale destruction of large areas
of the Bay and the displacement of much of its community.
The 1970s and '80s saw a new influx of refugees from con-
flicts around the world, in particular the long-running civil
wars in Somalia (Cardiff now has the largest Somali community in Britain).

The '90s witnessed the 'renewal' of the area as a leisure and business hotspot (which meant another wave of local residents being moved out). Tiger Bay had, in truth, been an archaic term for years, but the area was still known to most as 'Butetown', or simply 'the Docks'. Now, though, these terms gave way to 'Cardiff Bay', or its short form of 'the Bay'. Today, going 'down the Docks' has been replaced by going 'down the Bay'.

'The Bay' was the brainchild of Nicholas Edwards, when he was Welsh Secretary in the Thatcher government (1979–87). He thought that the area could be transformed

A mum with her children at the Butetown Carnival.

in a similar way to London's Docklands. The Cardiff Bay Development Corporation (CBDC) was set up to plough through the changes. And they did have to be 'ploughed through', as they were opposed by many locals, as well as residents of other parts of Cardiff (particularly Riverside, Pontcanna and Canton), who were worried about the possible increased risk of flooding from the River Taff. One of the main opponents was the Cardiff West MP Rhodri Morgan, who went on to become, some years later, First Minister of Wales. But by the time he had *that* job, Cardiff Bay was an established reality.

Today, the area has been transformed by the Cardiff Barrage, a sophisticated coastal lock that impounds the River Taff and the River Ely (the mouths of the two rivers are only half a mile apart) to create a massive freshwater lake. Along the quayside now are no sailors unloading ships. Instead we have a waterfront that features an array of restaurants, two yacht clubs and new luxury apartments in private estates with names like Mermaid Quay. As well as being a place where Cardiffians (and some day-trippers from outside Cardiff) like to go on a Sunday afternoon, it is also, during the week, a busy administrative centre.

The now-defunct South Glamorgan County Council moved to the Bay in the late '80s, and that is where Cardiff County Council has been based since it began work in the mid-'90s. When the Welsh Assembly was set up a few years later, that also was built 'down the Bay'. Now we also have the Wales Millennium Centre, a major cultural centre which houses, as well as concert halls, a network of offices where the 'movers and shakers' of the Welsh arts scene hold court.

There is also the council's much-touted 'international sports village'. This has not been such a resounding success, since none of the city's major rugby, football or cricket clubs have yet been lured into taking up a new home 'down the Bay', despite, in some cases, considerable inducement. Nevertheless, this sports village thing offers an international swimming pool (which also features a fun pool), a relocated ice rink (which hasn't quite been built yet) and a white-water canoeing centre.

Finally: Cardiff Bay features places called Mermaid Quay, Lloyd George Avenue and Atlantic Wharf. Sadly – and probably deliberately – it has no place which retains the name Tiger Bay. But if you stroll along Bute Street today, or nip off it into Loudoun Square, you can still catch a flavour of this unique Cardiff kaleidoscope of bygone days. Almost gone, maybe, but most definitely not forgotten.

ELY: A HAMLET BY A BRIDGE

Ely in Olden Times

Ely is a large and sprawling area, mainly comprised of council and former council houses, which forms the western extremity of Cardiff.

It takes its name from the River Ely. This runs down from hills near the Rhondda Valley, winds its way through the Vale of Glamorgan, and then empties into Cardiff Bay. It is believed that, in prehistoric times (at least as early as the seventh century BC), Celtic tribesmen sailed up the river from the Bay, looking for somewhere to settle. The place where Ely Bridge is located was a major landmark even then. That spot was where the river tended to silt up, and hence it was the first convenient place to ford it.

The Celts needed security in those times of tribal war, and so they built a hill fort, high up on a hill overlooking the surrounding countryside, from where they could spy the approach of enemy tribes. This area later became known as Caerau, after the Welsh word for 'forts'. This spot (St Mary's Hill) still affords an impressive view of the sprawling city beneath.

The main road going through Ely is today known as Cowbridge Road West, and is part of the A48. This road has a long history. Its route through Ely is almost 'as old as the hills', having been used as a trackway by the Celts in the Iron Age. When the Romans came, they used it as the route for part of their great military road from Gloucester to Neath.

The road and the Ely Bridge, probably first built by the Romans, continued to be the area's defining feature. By 1800, mail coaches were crossing the bridge on their way to Cowbridge (and thence to the port of Milford Haven), and so the bridge had to be rebuilt and the road – which was still just a cart track – widened and improved. It became a turnpike road, with the turnpike house located halfway between Amroth Road and Caerau Lane. Tolls were collected there until 1889; sadly, the house was demolished in 1930.

Although the road was improved after 1800, it did not run through any major conurbation – far from it! West of Canton Cross, a large stretch of wild and rugged fields – known as Ely Common – was all that existed, until you reached Ely Bridge.

And what of the territory west of the bridge? Well, at the time of the 1841 census, Ely was still a fairly sparsely populated area of only 224 residents. Most of these were Welsh-speaking farm labourers, working at farms that helped feed the town of Cardiff. Then, as the whole of Cardiff was transformed by the Industrial Revolution, Ely likewise underwent a dramatic change of character.

The Growth of Ely

In 1850, the South Wales Railway opened, running from Chepstow to Swansea. A station was set up at Ely (on the Fairwater side of Ely Bridge) and this soon became an important transport location – or 'hub', to use the current term. It was a major factor in David Davies opening a brewery at Ely Bridge (1855) and in Brown and Evans starting up Ely Paper Mill (1865). In 1855, Ely Racecourse opened a stone's throw away. Ely Bridge suddenly became a hive of industry.

As workers flooded into the area to staff the new enterprises, other amenities were set up there. Ely Mill, just up Mill Road, was taken over by the Cardiff Corporation and became Ely Pumping Station, guaranteeing a clean water supply – vital after the town had suffered a cholera epidemic in 1849. Ely Hospital also opened nearby and later there was an Ear, Nose and Throat Hospital. This stood next to the Children's Hospital – a homely looking affair whose front garden was adorned for years by a large model of the Old Lady's Shoe (from the nursery rhyme: 'There was an old lady who lived in a shoe / She had so many children, she didn't know what to do …').

The paper mill became, by 1900, the largest supplier of newspapers in the UK; for years, millions read the *Daily Express* every day, printed on paper from Ely Paper Mill. Ely Racecourse hosted the Welsh Grand National until 1939. Later, a second brewery – Crosswells – was set up at Ely Bridge, on the other side of the railway line from the first brewery, as well as a Chivers factory (Chivers made jams and pickles).

There were sidings leading from Ely station to the paper mill and to the brewery; on race days, the station would be exceptionally busy, bringing horses and jockeys along, as well as race-goers. Many travellers in western parts of Cardiff would get on the Paddington–Fishguard 'main line' at Ely station, rather than go into central Cardiff.

At the same time, Canton was changing, too. It began to expand westward on to Ely Common and, in 1897, one of Cardiff's showpiece parks – Victoria Park – opened. Further housing developments west of the park meant that Ely Common at some point disappeared entirely from view – I suppose the park itself is, in a way, the last remnant of the common. Eventually, Canton and Ely were linked by an almost continuous line of shops and houses, stretching from Canton Cross all the way up to Ely Bridge.

And west of the bridge, there was more of the same. By 1922, Cardiff's centre had become too clogged up with houses and people, and the 'slums' needed to be cleared. More room was therefore needed for the city to expand at its outer fringes. This was part of a national drive by Prime Minister David Lloyd George to build 'Homes for Heroes', for veterans returning from the First World War.

The city's boundary now moved west: the Corporation taking over the parish of Llandaff, which included Ely, as well as the further-outlying parishes of Caerau and Michaelston-super-Ely. There followed a busy few years of house-building as 'the Ely estate' was constructed. One of the earliest streets was Caerau Square, which was so badly built that it had to be demolished just forty year later. (Cymric Close and St David's Crescent were then built on the site.) This blunder aside, though, the houses were good. The oldest surviving houses were built in the Archer Road area: they were large – with gardens! Much better than the kind of housing that most ordinary people had known before.

These council houses were highly prized at the time, and this part of Ely was initially known as 'Ely Garden Suburb'. (This name has been revived in recent years by a local community group, which does sterling work in that area.) The next major stage of development was in the Amroth Road area. Eventually, by the time it had been completed after the Second World War, Ely was one of the largest housing developments in Western Europe.

A persistent problem was the regular flooding of the River Ely. This affected the paper mill, whose owners in 1948 successfully sued Cardiff Corporation for compensation. The council reacted by straightening the river, and the flooding problem was thereafter resolved.

Ely Paper Mill was like a self-enclosed community, which had its own internal railway system, an open-air swimming pool where wives and children of mill workers could go on hot summer days (the mill also had its own successful swimming team), and a monthly community newspaper.* Several generations of Ely families worked there. It was one of the first places in Cardiff to introduce shift work, and had a loud hooter that would signal the beginning and end of shifts.

There were environmental drawbacks to having the paper mill. With little knowledge of health and safety, one of the local features was 'seeing the river change colour' every so often, as dye from the paper-making process was emptied into it. Thankfully, the River Ely is looking a little better these days.

Alas, the industry around Ely Bridge went into decline. The racecourse never recovered from having its two stands burned down in a fire in 1937, and held its last race – won by Keith Piggott (Lester Piggott's father) – in April 1939. Racing never resumed there after the war, and the Welsh 'National' ultimately switched to Chepstow.

The train station closed in 1963. The same year, the original Ely 'Tower' Brewery shut its doors as the two breweries merged. Within twenty years, the second brewery had also gone, to be replaced by a housing development. The brewery

*Ely Garden Villagers hold an 'Elympics' every year, a competitive sports day for junior school kids, and run the Cardiff Hibernian football teams.

offices, built on the site of the old Ely Cattle Market, became part of Fairwater Police Station. The Chivers factory pickled its last jar in 1980. Finally, Ely Paper Mill closed in 1999.

Place Names
Ely, up to the Second World War and for some time afterwards, straddled the river. As well as Ely station, Ely Ales' Tower Brewery and Ely Cattle Market (in Norbury Road) were on the 'Fairwater' side of the river – although most of Fairwater hadn't been built yet. Eventually, when a large-scale council-housing development was built there, everything on the east side of the river became 'Fairwater', with 'Ely' meaning, to most people, everything west of the bridge. (Mind you, during the '90s, the Railway pub on the east side was still listed by Brains brewery as being in 'Ely'. Discuss ...)

Just west of the bridge – by where the Ely Royal Air Force Association (RAFA) Club now stands – was an area known as 'Riverside' (the main street is still called Riverside Terrace). This is one of three 'Riversides' in Cardiff, as there is a 'Riverside' area adjacent to each of the city's three rivers. (The fields by the River Rumney, where Rumney Rugby Club play, are known as 'Riverside Fields'.

And, of course, there is 'Riverside' by the Taff, opposite the rugby stadium.)

Over the next few years, the new Ely estate moved relentlessly westwards, until it reached Culverhouse Cross, a major road junction that now signifies the westernmost point of Cardiff. From Ely Bridge to Culverhouse Cross was a distance of almost 3 miles; today this area is home to almost 25,000 residents.

In spreading this far west, Ely eventually swallowed up the old villages of Caerau and Michaelston-super-Ely. Caerau village had developed around its farmhouse, which later – with the spread of Ely – became the Highfields pub, part of a busy new shopping parade. Michaelston, further west again, was less intensely developed until much more recently.

Another name that has been used in Ely is 'Trelai', as in 'Heol Trelai' and 'Trelai Park', the official name for what used to be Ely Racecourse. Trelai, as a name, was probably invented in the early 1900s as an attempt to 'Welshify' the name 'Ely', Trelai meaning 'town on the Ely'. Most local historians are doubtful, though, if this name was ever used by the original Welsh-speaking residents of Ely.

Eventually, this whole area, Ely, became so highly populated that the council had to split it into two electoral wards (voting districts): 'Ely', north of Cowbridge Road, and 'Caerau', south of it. Many residents of the southern half now follow the council's initiative by calling themselves residents of 'Caerau', rather than 'Ely'.

Some of the residents of Michaelston have pulled a stranger trick. As there are now more of them than there are of residents from the old village of St Fagans on the other side of the river, the St Fagans primary school has shifted into a newer building in Michaelston. So social-climbing Michaelstonians tell people they live in St Fagans!

However, these complex delineations only really matter to people living west of Ely Bridge. To people living east of the bridge, it is all simply 'Ely'.

Pubs and Clubs

Nearly all of the pubs that were in Ely twenty years ago are now closed or have a different name. Just over the bridge were two pubs almost next door to one another: the Bridge Inn (recently closed) and the White Lion (closed down by the police for rowdiness in the '90s), which is now flats. The authorities had already closed down the Dusty Forge, a mile or two further along the main road, for similar reasons: this is now a young-people's training centre. The 'Dusty', in the dim and distant past, had been next door to a blacksmith's and may have been used as an unofficial stopping-off point for coaches whose horses needed to be reshod.

The last pub on the main road was the Culverhouse. This was opened in the '30s, next door to an earlier stone cottage-type pub, the Caerau Arms, which closed to make way for 'the Culver'. The name of the Culverhouse referred to the nearby Culverhouse Farm in Michaelston. A culverhouse (or dovecote) is a place where birds are kept, and at this farm, pigeons and doves would be bred and fattened

for eating. These days the pub is called Cooper's Carvery. Not quite as romantic, eh?

In the side streets, on the Caerau side of the main road, were two other pubs. The Highfields was mentioned earlier; amazingly this still exists (as I write) and has the same name. Nearer Ely Bridge on Bishopstone Road was the Anthonys, named after two racing brothers who rode and trained winners at the nearby racecourse; this is now 'the Caerau'. Only, the original Caerau farmhouse was the Highfields, so if any pub should be called 'the Caerau', it's the Highfields. What was wrong with 'the Anthonys', anyway? Oh, never mind ...

Clubs include the RAFA Club (near Ely Bridge); the Ely Sports & Social (formerly the Royal British Legion Club) and Ely Cons, both on the main road; the Cardiff West End Social Club, further west; and on Heol Trelai, the Home Guard Club. There is also a 'hidden' pub. Years ago the Hancocks brewery pub was the Red Lion, tucked away in a side street just off Ely Bridge. In the '90s, this became the highly mysterious Coach House. Apparently it's a pub, and it's open, but I've tried to go there three or four times and every time it's been shut. Weird. You try it!

An Interesting Walk

Up St Mary's Hill lies Cwrt-yr-Ala Park, where another housing estate has been added in the last twenty years. If you walk up Cwrt-yr-Ala Road and through the estate, you go past the football ground, and – suddenly – you have left behind the streets of the city and entered the serenity of the countryside. You can continue across the fields (along decent footpaths), past the sleepy hamlet of Michaelston-le-Pit with its shady duck pond, to Dinas Powys. On a sunny day, it's rural bliss. And there are pubs in Dinas ...

RHIWBINA: CARDIFF'S GARDEN VILLAGE

Many parts of this book celebrate life in the older, inner-city parts of Cardiff. The likes of Grangetown, Splott and Canton.

But the more affluent, suburban areas of the city also boast a colourful and interesting history.

In the north of the city, the first houses in the grandly named Rhiwbina Garden Village were completed in 1913. To this day, the area – despite many additions – has managed to retain the ageless semi-rural charm created so long ago.

Rhiwbina derives its name from St Beuno, a seventh-century holy man from Gwynedd. The name 'Rhiwbina' translates as 'St Beuno's hill'. The place itself was part of a national 'garden city' (or 'garden suburb') movement, which gripped the town planners of England and Wales just after the turn of the century. The thinking at the time was to recreate the success of garden villages springing up in England (such as Letchworth and Welwyn Garden City in Hertfordshire, and Bournville in Birmingham) and offer industrial workers simple homes with gardens, fresh air and plenty of space.

What made these kind of suburbs possible was the coming of the railways. The Cardiff Railway Company had opened a line linking the docks with the Valley lines, and Rhiwbina had a station (opened in 1911). Once passenger trains started chugging along the line, as well as goods trains, the scene was set fair for another chunk of 'suburbia' to be built.

The new housing development sounded wonderful. The 1913 prospectus for the Rhiwbina Garden Village said: 'There is no dismal little backyard, but everything is free and open – and habits of neatness and cleanliness are at once acquired.'

Yes, this outlying suburb was meant for the workers. There was a definite idea of improving the 'habits' of these blue-collared men, who were not expected to continue

their previous practice of drinking many pots of beer. So Rhiwbina, like most of the other garden cities, did not include any pubs in its plans. A fatal error?

The new garden suburb was based on a master plan by Sir Raymond Unwin, one of the leading architects of the garden city movement. The first thirty-four houses appeared in 1913, and more were built from 1919 to 1923, occupying an area between Pen-y-dre and Lon Isa.

The community was to be run as a co-operative by Rhiwbina Garden Village Society, with residents renting their properties. Formed in 1912, the company was originally called the 'Cardiff Worker's Co-operative Garden Village Society Ltd', but this not exactly snappy monicker was changed soon afterwards, to the 'Rhiwbina Garden Village Ltd'.

Each of the first thirty-four houses was supplied with water, gas for cooking and lighting, a boiler, a water-storage tank and a dustbin. Fences, hedges and paths followed. Some of these features, which householders would later take for granted, were new innovations at the time – at least for the working classes.

The idea was for the village to have grass verges, so as to give the workers the impression of the countryside, and a back garden for children to play. Alas, the idealistic notion of providing a lot of green space for 'the workers' was never really achieved, as rents proved beyond the means of the city's labouring classes. (Most of them, in truth, were not that keen to leave their closely knit neighbourhoods of terraces, pubs and shops, in any case.) Instead, Rhiwbina became what it has been ever since, a honey-pot for the aspiring – and fairly affluent – middle-class professionals.

The 'village' soon gained a reputation for boasting a number of distinguished academics, as well as popular Welsh historical novelist Jack Jones, another author in Kate Roberts, playwright Tom Richards and the actress Rachel Thomas, who was forever playing the stereotypical 'Welsh mam'. Oddly, in the '60s, Rhiwbina did become home for some of the (former) working classes, as it became a popular residence for many Cardiff City footballers. John Charles, Alan Harrington, Brian Clark and others lived there. By this time, the area had outgrown the original garden village – and there were pubs. Many of the City players would converge on the Butchers Arms for beer and darts on Friday nights.

This beer-drinking pastime would have had Raymond Unwin turning in his grave. But things were changing in Rhiwbina. In the '60s, the long-established rental arrangement finally came to an end, and the tenants were able, for the first time, to buy their own homes. By now, many more privately owned homes were also being built in the area.

Today, Rhiwbina Garden Village is perhaps the best example of a garden suburb scheme in Wales. In 1977, the area was declared a conservation area, and most of the houses now enjoy listed-building status.

Until the 1980s, Rhiwbina was pretty much the northern-most point of Cardiff. Then the new estate of Thornhill was added, tucked away in the last available pocket of land between the city and the M4 motorway. But, despite this addition, Rhiwbina retains a rural feel. It is close to the large green spaces of Whitchurch Golf Club and to Thornhill Crematorium. Just up the hill, there is the Wenallt, a pleasant wooded area, which affords fine views of the city. From there, one can wander up to places like Caerphilly and Rudry.

An alternative is to walk 'the green line', a footpath snak-ing its way through small green areas tucked in between various northern suburbs. From Rhiwbina, you can go through Llanishen and Thornhill and end up in Lisvane. A session at the Griffin Inn is a good climax to this walk.

There are three pubs in the Rhiwbina area: the Nine Giants, on Caerphilly Road; the Deri in Heol-y-Deri, at the bottom of Rhiwbina Hill; and the very pleasant Butchers Arms, tucked away in a little oasis of green by the brook. There is much knowledge of both the city's football and rugby teams in this place, and the pool table must be the fastest in Cardiff – and the locals some of the 'meanest' players!

SPLOTT. WHERE TO EVEN START?

It would be difficult to construct any kind of commentary on Cardiff without a section on Splott. For, while many places could be said to be the home of the 'real' Cardiff, Splott is, or maybe was, a law unto itself. Some newer suburbs of Cardiff may display a lack of character or present that could-be-anywhere feeling, but the long dark streets of Splott tell a unique and colourful tale.

To the uninitiated, Splott lies between Roath and the Bristol Channel. The housing is largely Victorian in character, supplemented by more recent pockets of social housing. Immediately to the west of Splott sits the tiny housing estate of Tremorfa, a kind of dormitory town that once housed many of the workers from the heavy industry that gave Splott it's raison d'être.

Amazingly, Tremorfa once had its own airport, a civilian airfield that was also sometimes known as Splott Aerodrome. The nearby 'Old Airport' pub though is, like the airport itself, long gone.

It's easy enough to research the history of somewhere like Splott. You can quickly discover that, say, Splott Park dates from 1901, that Shirley Bassey attended Moorland Road School or that Splott even had its own university. You can read conflicting debates about the origin of the name and participate in online disputes about whether Pearl Street or even the old Splott Cinema was in Splott, Roath or Adamsdown. Highly readable books about Splott emerged many years ago to help you with all this, such as The Splott I Knew *by the late Bill Phillips.*

But really, it's a place where you have to walk the streets.

In very early times, Splott was unofficially divided into Upper and Lower Splott. A ladder of around sixteen or so humble streets later made up 'Lower Splott' – a title derived from the days when the area comprised merely two patches of land at Upper Splott and Lower Splott Farms. This was long before the vast East Moors steelworks began to billow its sulphur and smoke over the adjoining rows of tightly knit terraced houses.

People from 'Lower Splott' didn't really enjoy that title by the way. It always implied some sort of inferiority compared to 'Upper Splott', which was slightly further north. Instead, people down there described themselves as being from 'Down the Bottom'.

On the other hand, Upper Splott was positively genteel compared to the Dickensian atmosphere of Down the Bottom, where policemen travelled in pairs and ragged children of all races kicked footballs against bare walls, before being commanded to 'go play up your own end' by angry mothers mounting their endless battle to keep the thick, grey steelwork's smog off the window panes.

Life was, at times, extremely tough here. A famous photograph from the 1930s depicts 'The Soup Time' outside Splott Labour Hall in Neath Street. Even in my childhood there during the 1960s, hand-made clothes or toys made by your uncle seemed entirely normal.

Row upon row of featureless Victorian properties ran parallel to one another down the spine of Lower Splott, until Robinson Square intervened to break up the bleak street pattern. Then the terraces continued – Enid Street, Layard Street and, eventually, Menalaus Street, at the very end of the line. The end of the world even.

Hinton Street formed an unofficial boundary between the streets of Lower Splott, named after Welsh towns like Tenby, Llanelli and even Swansea, and the wider, calmer avenues of Upper Splott, where some streets were even lined with trees.

Hinton Street had corner shops on three of its four corners and still faces Moorland Road School across a scruffy little park, officially known as Moorland Gardens. Within a short walk lay imposing pubs such as the enormous Grosvenor, the Wimbourne or the unique Bomb & Dagger – exactly as it sounds by the way. These were establishments the like of which you simply do not see these days. No room here for two-for-one Valentines Day meals. Characters like 'Gunslinger', 'Shoecobbler' and the creepy 'Cecil' added further to the sense of notoriety.

But Lower Splott didn't have a monopoly on all the colour and character. Splott School, on Splott Road, was an enormous, black centre of excellence that stood on the site of the current STAR Centre and Splott Bridge takes you back to the real world across the Swansea to Paddington railway line. From here you can still walk the length of Railway Street to another bridge at Beresford Road without crossing a pavement.

Splott boasts a rich sporting heritage. Somewhere I have a photograph of my father in the baseball kit of Splott YMCA, while the local football teams included Bridgend St Mission FC. Bridgend Street featured a church, or 'mission', at the far end near the steelworks. Splott stalwarts like Theo Bowley and Pop Bowley preached fire and brimstone here and ran the football team, which continues to play in red and white stripes. Even today, the club's motto is 'Deeds not Words', a common theme in Scripture, and if you visit the club's current Welsh League ground in nearby Tremorfa, you will still hear the cry 'come on The Mish …'

Yet Splott is nothing if not ecumenical. Further up the myriad of terraced houses sits St Albans RC church. This colossal venue would not be out of place in York or Bath. It also lends its name to St Albans AFC and a rugby club. This doesn't quite put things on a Rangers/Celtic level but the Mission's humble, Nonconformist 'chapel' roots contrast sharply with the mighty St Albans Cathedral on Habershon Street. The football team's kit was, and I think still is, yellow and black stripes.

Before supermarkets were invented, the weekly 'proper shop' took place across a range of tiny retail outlets crammed the length of the long, long Portmanmoor Road. It was possible to buy anything in Portmanmoor Road. It housed The Fleurs social club – the only remaining evidence of the street's existence – two pubs, a post office, and what felt like dozens of shops selling groceries, meat and newspapers. One shop sold sweets. Just sweets.

I guess this all sounds quite sentimental if you now shop at Sainsburys in Thornhill, but life really was like this. The whole world was on the doorstep. Residents would queue to use the red phone box in Walker Road, buy chips on the corner opposite The Ruperra pub and hang out the washing every Monday, hoping that, for once, it wouldn't come back dirtier than it went out. Coal was delivered to the back door and the pop man brought Dandelion & Burdock to the front door. If us kids fancied a glimpse of the magical, we would wander up Splott Road to gaze longingly through the windows of Youngs, a wonderful Shangri-La of an establishment that sold toys. Just toys. And I am not talking pre-war here, for East Moors steelworks didn't shut until 1978.

Splott is a different place now. Long rows of chimney pots still sprinkle the skyline as its cramped streets hunt desperately for any tiny patch of green. But these days many people pass through Splott – or at least around it – en route to the refurbished watery environment of Cardiff Bay. Modern commercial premises clutter around its perimeter and the population today totals around 12,000. The culture of the place has changed but its place in the history of the city is secure. It was fierce yet friendly, warm yet wild, dark yet dazzling.

It was, and is, proper Cardiff.

TOP TEN CARDIFF PARKS

1. Parc Cefn Onn
Almost a hidden gem in the northern suburb of Lisvane. Go in May when the azaleas and rhododendrons are in bloom. Rest awhile alongside the fishpond. Enjoy a picnic on the grassy slopes overlooking the city. Almost paradise.

2. Roath Park
Row a boat, feed the ducks, go on the swings or the bumpy slide, play on the grass. Next time the kids want to go somewhere expensive, like 10-pin bowling, take them to Roath Park instead.

3. Bute Park
An enormous green lung bringing a vast and leafy open space down to the very walls of Cardiff Castle.

4. Pontcanna Fields
Home to 1,000 football pitches, it adjoins Bute Park and Llandaff Fields, which was one of several parks to once feature an open-air pool.

5. Thompsons Park
A tiny jewel in the labyrinth of Canton streets.

6. Grange Gardens
Ditto but insert 'Grangetown' for 'Canton'.

7. Splott Park
Once home to the infamous Splott Baths and Jessie the train. Still worth walking about in now, mind. Sports pitches, a bowling green and a children's play area feature here.

8. Victoria Park

Another legendary Cardiff attraction. This park includes a free open-air paddling pool and more ice cream than you can shake a stick at.

9. The Glider Fields, *Llanishen*

Discover football pitches alongside a skatepark and leisure centre. There is even a pub across the road. You could take your holidays here and save yourself a fortune.

10. The Marl, *Grangetown*

Practically in the sea, this one. Take a windbreak.

6

GOING
OUT

This chapter is all about what Cardiffians have done over the years when they have gone out for the night. The first thing to realise is that Cardiff was an industrial city, built on the toil of workers, many of whom had simple pleasures. The simplest pleasure of all was to go into a pub and down a pint of beer. So, before I tackle the many other forms of night-time entertainment which Cardiff has offered, I must scribble down something about the city's major preoccupation for many years: **going to the pub**.

WE'RE GOING DOWN THE PUB!

Now, David has touched on this subject in his praise of Brains brewery in the Food and Drink chapter. But I want to delve a little deeper than that.

Brains now tends to be regarded as an iconic Cardiff company. It is only in fairly recent times, though, that they have been Cardiff's only city-based brewery. Cardiff used to have several.

BRAINS' 'SURGERIES'

Brains brewers trace their heritage back to around 1800, when James Walters began making beer on the site of what later became known as 'the Old Brewery' in St Mary Street.

This is the site that is now known as 'the Old Brewery Quarter'. Younger readers (if there are any reading this) have to imagine that for years this place was a brewery, with delivery lorries trundling in and out of an entrance which gave on to St Mary Street. Strange but true!

Right, back to Walters and his Old Brewery (although it wasn't called that until later). As Cardiff expanded over the next fifty years, there was a boom in population – and a boom in brewing. Until Gladstone's government of 1869, pubs did not really even need a licence to begin business. So there were innumerable pubs sprouting up, some of them in people's houses, and these pubs often made their own beer. But customers began to complain about the variability of the beer, and many pub owners realised that they needed to be supplied by a proper brewery.

The Old Brewery was one of many breweries that opened in Cardiff in this era. John Walters sold up and it changed hands several times. In 1882, the Thomas Brothers sold it on to their brother-in-law. He was a bright young man from a rich Gloucestershire family, who was trying to make his way in the world of Cardiff brewing. His name was Samuel Arthur (S.A.) Brain.

At this time, there were still at least half a dozen different breweries in Cardiff. Sam Brain was previously the manager of a rival firm, the Phoenix Brewery. This eventually became Hancocks, but there will be more on them later.

WOT – NO BEER?!

A major landmark for the brewers came with the Sunday Closing (Wales) Act of 1881. Some brewers feared this piece of government meddling was the beginning of the end for pubs.

The Act was passed after the election, in 1880, of another Liberal government under Gladstone. The 'Liberals' (who were not liberal at all when it came to beer) were closely associated with the Methodists and the chapels. Many of the chapels were involved in campaigns against what they saw as 'the demon drink', and were backing various forms of 'temperance'. Temperance is supposed to mean the individual abstaining from doing naughty things – like drinking beer. In political terms, it meant banning people from drinking.

When the Liberals got in again in 1880, they immediately sought to appease their pals in the chapels by bringing in 'temperance'. When they tried to introduce a Temperance Act for England, it was rejected by Parliament. But they managed to pass the Sunday Closing (Wales) Act in 1881, forcing all pubs in Wales to stay shut on Sundays.

In Cardiff, this Act panicked the Thomas Brothers into selling their business to Sam Brain. Many brewers thought it sounded the death knell for the pub trade. After all, we already had an area near the train station and rugby stadium (Temperance Town) where all pubs, off-licences and hotel bars were totally forbidden because landowner Colonel Wood was a 'temperance' man. Might this kind of prohibition be extended, in time, to the whole of Cardiff? (In the USA, it eventually applied to the whole country.)

Hardened drinkers were worried too! But luckily for them, there were some loopholes. One was that the Act did not apply to private members' clubs, resulting in lots of clubs starting up. Another oddity was that Monmouthshire was not covered by the Act.

(Now, this Monmouthshire aspect is a bit strange, and seems to be tied up with Parliament not being too sure at this time if Monmouthshire was in England or in Wales. It seems that in this pre-First World War period, the Rhymney River may have been not only the **county border** between Glamorgan and Monmouthshire, but was also considered to be the **regional border** between England and Wales.)

Drinkers took many routes to bypass the Sunday clos-ing laws over the years. One was, as already mentioned, drinking in clubs. Another idea was to go across the Rhymney River into England and have a pint there. But Monmouthshire only remained outside the Sunday Closing Act until 1915. Then, wartime restrictions made that county 'dry' on Sundays as well. This was confirmed by another Act in 1921, which made Sunday licensing in Monmouth exactly the same as that in the rest of Wales. It might now be considered that it was this 1921 Act that finally stated that Monmouth was in Wales and not in England!

Enough of Monmouthshire, and back to Cardiff. There was no way that the residents of Tiger Bay were going to be stopped from drinking on Sundays, so unofficial clubs sprouted in people's houses, known as 'shebeens' (an Irish word). There was also 'the Club de Marl', where Bob Downey, the landlord of the Bute Castle pub, ran an open-air Sunday drinking club on a patch of waste ground. (No good if it rained, mind.)

The crazy situation of Wales having totally different Sunday licensing laws to England persisted until 1961. Then the Sunday Closing Act was repealed by the Licensing Act. This introduced a local ballot in each district council area, to be held every five years, which would decide whether or not the area would remain 'dry' on a Sunday. Cardiff imme-diately opted to be 'wet'.

By the 1990s, only the Welsh-speaking, God-fearing chapel-goers of Dwyfor in Caernarfonshire were still intent on staying 'dry'; Dwyfor was then abolished in the next round of local government reorganisation in 1993. Since 2003, there has been no need to hold any ballots in Wales on this issue – and none of Wales is dry on Sundays.

BRAINS GET BIGGER

The Sunday closing laws did not, then, spell the beginning of the end for brewing in Cardiff. There was another 'Temperance Town', because when Rhiwbina was developed as a 'garden village' in the early 1900s, pubs were initially banned there, too. But everywhere else in Cardiff, people carried on drinking.

Sam Brain then began to seriously develop the brewery he had bought. In 1887, the Old Brewery expanded from its relatively small operation behind the Albert pub into a much larger affair. Around the same time, Brains also acquired a maltings in East Moors. (Note: a maltings is a place where grain is converted into malt. The malt is then used to make beer at another place, called a brewery. Later, maltings and breweries often tended to be located next to one another in adjacent buildings.)

In those days, 'town' was not full of nightclubs and 'bars', but full of places that were just – pubs. Queen Street had several. St Mary Street had a stack of them, including four in a row, side by side, near the corner with Mill Lane: the Royal Oak, the Blue Anchor, Elliott's Hotel and the Terminus (the last of the four is still a bar, now called the Pepperpot Lounge).

After the First World War, there were more changes for Brains. The brewery opened a bottling plant at Nora Street in Roath. They also switched their delivery vehicles from horse-drawn carriages called drays, to steam wagons. But many of the old 'draymen' preferred the old methods. There was a tradition that the drayman got a free pint in each pub he delivered to, and some draymen would fall asleep at the reins towards the end of their shift. No matter, though, in the horse-drawn drays, as the experienced horses knew the route home on their own!

The steam wagons were essentially designed to carry more beer, so that the draymen could cover more pubs in one round. They proved to be only a temporary mode of transport, though, and were replaced during the 1930s by the petrol-fuelled lorries that we still have today.

BOOZING AFTER THE WAR

Brains became well known after the war for their advertising on Cardiff buses and on railway bridges. But getting these adverts displayed was, for many years, a problem, with advertising bans being intermittently enforced by the city council and the Great Western Railway. As late as 1932, we had a 'temperance' man serving as Lord Mayor – one Alderman Sanders – who banned booze from all civic events during his year in office. Eventually, though, these 'august bodies' calmed down and allowed the company to put these great adverts on display across the city.

In the late 1940s and '50s, drinking in pubs tended to revolve, in the evenings, around games like darts and skittles, cards and, in certain pubs, sing-songs around the piano. Pubs were divided into separate rooms. There was always a bar and a lounge (the latter for the smarter-dressed customers), while some pubs also had a third, smaller room called a 'snug bar' or 'smoke room'.

In this immediate post-war era, men would generally drink beer, as lager was a 'Continental' drink that was barely sold over here. The ladies would tend to drink shorter drinks like gin and tonic, gin and lemon or 'gin and It' ('It' being Italian vermouth).

The main beer drunk in Brains pubs in this era was Brains Dark. There was also a good trade in 'light-and-dark', which was dark mixed with light, a sort of drinkers' version of 'half-and-half'. (Another note: 'Light' is the old Cardiff

term for bitter. The use of this term has almost died out over the past thirty years.)

Bitter drinkers in those days were in a minority, and this persisted for many years. Dark was still Brains' best-seller until the early '80s, and some Brains pubs didn't even bother selling bitter. The Railway Hotel in Fairwater, for instance, sold only dark as late as 1980.

Brains trumpeted their dark during the '80s as a national prizewinner – it was voted Best British Mild in 1981. They then contradicted themselves in the '90s by phasing it out in most of their pubs, in favour of some chemicalised concoction called 'Dark Smooth', which was not the same thing at all. Now the habit of drinking dark is dying out, continued only by a few old blokes – and me, if I can find it anywhere. (I was converted to dark by the old blokes when I worked as a barman at the Butchers Arms in Canton.

They were right. It was the tastiest drink in the pub. Women like it, too, because it's made of caramel.)

Now even bitter – which gradually took over from dark as the Cardiff 'workingman's drink' – is not drunk by many. Some 90 per cent of blokes in Cardiff pubs these days drink lager. When I was a stripling in the '80s, there were still many males who regarded this newfangled stuff as 'a woman's drink'. But now it is obvious that lager has won the day, and beer drinking has become almost a niche activity, to be perpetuated by members of Camra – which in the '80s was almost a secret society, like the Freemason's. To me, though, dark is a tidy drink, bitter is a decent drink and lager is all gas!

Of course, a problem now is that so few people drink the bitter that it goes stale in the barrel. So a pint of bitter is now extremely variable, except in very busy pubs. Because the beer has become so erratic in quality, more beer-drinkers have gone 'over to the other side' and started drinking lager. Lager, at least, is fairly consistent – you know what you are getting. So less people drink the beer, which gets even more variable, and the vicious circle continues.

Now, to go back to this business of lager being 'a woman's drink'. In the 1960s and '70s, things like Babycham and Cinzano started taking over from the old gin drinks as the popular beverages for the ladies. By the 1980s, a 'half of lager' had come in. Yes, girls only drank 'halves' then – it was very rare to see women drinking pints of beer. The ones who did tended to be girls you wouldn't want to 'mess about' with.

I have rambled over a few points here, and got away from one of the issues I wanted to develop, which was that Brains was not the only brewery in Cardiff. My generation of drinkers may be in danger of not even realising this.

There is a clue to this in what David mentioned, in passing, in his piece about Brains: he said it was actually

Allbright that was 'the beer of my youth'. And you certainly did not get Allbright Bitter in Brains pubs.

When I began drinking in earnest in the late '80s, I knew my father as 'a Brains man'. He didn't like to go in pubs if they weren't Brains. (This confused me, because to me, a pub was a pub. A pub means beer. What else mattered?) But, oddly, I later discovered that my father had been reared, in his youth, not on Brains, but on Hancocks HB.

HB and Allbright Bitter both hint at something that is in danger of being forgotten. Once upon a time, Brains was not *the* Cardiff brewery. There were two 'biggies': one was Brains and the other was Hancocks.

HANDS OFF SOCKS, ON HANCOCKS

Hancocks Brewery began in Wiveliscombe, a small market town in Somerset. But Hancocks needed a bigger market for their beers than small places in the rural West Country, so they began shipping the stuff over from Minehead to busy industrial South Wales. Then, as their operation got bigger, they started up breweries on this side of the Bristol Channel. By 1900, Hancock's had established such facilities in Newport, Cardiff and Swansea – and they owned many pubs in all three places. (Unlike Brains, which never really broke out of Cardiff until very recent times.)

Hancocks had also moved their Cardiff brewery from Working Street (near the Hayes) to a newly built 'tower' brewery just south of Cardiff General railway station, in Penarth Road. This was their Cardiff nerve centre for the next seventy years.

Hancocks brewed beers like Amber Ale, Nut Brown Ale and their popular bitter, HB (Hancocks Best). Their symbol was a jolly John Bull figure brandishing a foaming pint of ale at arm's length. The Hancocks brewery was a village in itself, with plenty of facilities for the workers, including a dance hall, billiard room, library, table tennis, darts, a gymnasium and rifle range. It is a wonder that anybody ever made it home after work!

For years, Hancocks and Brains were the main rivals in Cardiff. Outside the city, Hancocks had many pubs in the Vale, Merthyr and the Valleys, as well as in Newport and Swansea. Brains had none of this. But Hancocks eventually got too big and during the '60s, an age when mergers created six 'giant' national brewers, Hancocks got swallowed up.

For years, Hancocks pubs had been the South Wales outlet for Worthington. This was made by one of the big brewers in Burton-on-Trent in the Midlands. (Burton was famous for its Trent waters, hence many brewers started up there.) But Worthington got taken over by Bass. Then Bass merged with Charrington and became Bass-Charrington, one of the biggest brewing operations in the country; Bass-Charrington then swallowed up Hancocks. The last Hancocks pub to open in Cardiff was the Master Gunner, on the Gabalfa estate, in 1967.

Fortunately for Hancocks drinkers, a bloke called Arwyn Owen was put in charge of Bass-Charrington's South Wales operation. He kept the pubs distinctly local in flavour and you could still buy a pint of Hancock's HB. The South Wales pubs also had their own company name, which was 'Welsh Brewers'.

We then had some marvellous TV ads over the next twenty years for their beers, using the slogan 'Never Forget Your Welsh'. The best one was a couple of blokes crawling through the desert, until they get to a sign that proclaimed, 'Welcome to Wales', and suddenly they enter a green, fertile valley. Finally they enter a lively, welcoming pub and begin downing pints of the beer that Welsh Brewers were so keen to promote: Allbright Bitter!

I say 'Allbright Bitter' with an exclamation mark, because this was perhaps one of the least potent brews in history. It was a typical 1970s keg beer, in that it seemed to possess no taste whatsoever, and its major property seemed to be that you could knock back four or five pints of the stuff and still feel more sober than when you'd left the house! But for many people, Allbright brings back great memories. And it was 'Allbright' which was emblazoned on the tower at the Penarth Road brewery for many years.

The Penarth Road operation seemed set to end in 1997, when Bass-Charrington announced they were concentrating their brewing in Burton. But Brains stepped in to buy the brewery from them, which was how Brains was able to leave the cramped 'Old Brewery' and turn it into today's 'Brewery Quarter'.

As for the Welsh Brewers (formerly Hancock's) pubs, well, there was a further merger, with Whitbread, which made the company too big. The government told them to sell off the Welsh Brewers operation, and all those pubs have now been taken over by other pub chains and independent licensees. So the idea of Hancocks pubs, which was perpetuated for thirty-five years by Welsh Brewers, has now almost entirely disappeared. There is no more Allbright. And though there is still a beer that calls itself HB, it seems to me to bear no relation in taste to the distinctively nutty flavour of the old HB. Even worse, it is now brewed, under licence, by Brains!

BREWERS' DROOP: THE MINOR BREWERS OF CARDIFF

There were at least two other fairly major brewers in Cardiff, even after the Second World War, both of them based in Ely.

The original brewery in Ely began operating in 1853, and was later known as 'Tower Brewery' (after the big brewery tower was built in 1936). It was bought in 1887 by a consortium of Welsh licensees who called their business the 'Ely Brewing Company'. Its pubs were commonly termed 'Ely Ales', after the advertising slogan 'Ely Ales, Best in Wales', and it had as its symbol a picture of Ely Bridge.

Ely Ales was only a relative minnow in Cardiff, but it did have some pubs further afield, in various Valleys towns. However, it was then taken over by a much bigger brewer from up the Valleys – Rhondda Valley Breweries, which took over Ely Ales in 1920. In Cardiff, though, pubs still sported the Ely Ales logos, and brewing carried on at the Tower Brewery by Ely Bridge.

However, 80 per cent of the Rhondda and Ely pubs were now up the Valleys, and this area, in the 1930s, went into serious economic decline. The company was soon on its knees. By the time the war ended, the Ely pubs in Cardiff were in a thoroughly dilapidated state.

The company was then brought back from the dead by the appropriately named Lazarus Nidditch, a heavily bespectacled businessman who managed to renovate the 'old men's pubs' and replace them with modern pubs boasting comfy lounges. The old Ely Bridge symbol was replaced by a barrel of Ely Ale. Trade revived, and in 1956 Ely even opened a new pub in Cardiff, the first one it had opened for decades: the New Ely in Cathays, which had the novelty of a ladies-only lounge.

Alas, the new prosperity attracted business 'hawks', and in 1959, after ruthless Cardiff speculator Julian Hodge made several attempts to hijack Ely, the company was forced to agree to a merger with Rhymney Breweries.

So who were Rhymney? Well, their story begins with Crosswells. This was a second company that decided to build a brewery at Ely Bridge – the water there was very good for brewing – and this area became Cardiff's little equivalent of Burton-on-Trent. Crosswells set up shop there in 1900, building their brewery – with stupendous cheek – just across the railway line from the Ely Ales Brewery.

Crosswells had begun life at Oldbury, near Birmingham, in 1887, but they were attracted by the number of thriving pubs in busy South Wales and relocated brewing operations to Ely Bridge. They had some pubs in Cardiff, sporting their beehive logo and delivering pints of their Crosswells Strong Ale, and also had interests in the city's wine and spirits trade. For some years, the big boss, Bill Tatem, was a prominent Cardiff shipowner – a rather dodgy character who later managed to become Lord Glanely.

Tatem sold the company at a big profit in 1936, to Rhymney Breweries from up the Valleys. The beehive logo went, to be replaced by Rhymney's hobbyhorse motif, and Crosswells beers soon disappeared from their old pubs. But brewing carried on at the Ely Bridge brewery.

Eventually, Rhymney swallowed up Ely in 1959, meaning there were two breweries within spitting distance of one another, both owned by the same company. In 1963 the Tower Brewery was knocked down by the same steeplejack who had built it twenty-five-odd years earlier. Rhymney carried on brewing at the old Crosswells brewery until 1982.

By this time, though, it was no longer just 'Rhymney', because it had been taken over by London brewer Whitbread. They had interests in Cardiff for many years, running a bottling plant at Penarth Road that supplied bottles to many South Wales pubs and Whitbread-owned off-licences. Finally, they bought Rhymney in 1965 and Whitbread became the third major player (along with Brains and Welsh Brewers) on the Cardiff pub scene.

Whitbread made a token attempt to keep a local flavour, by delivering a variable brew known as 'Welsh Bitter', a fairly soulless keg beer. When I was starting to drink, there were plenty of Whitbread pubs in Cardiff, but they had no real identity. The pump beer tended to be different in different pubs, although often – for a while, anyway – it was something called Flower's Original. But of the three big Cardiff brewers in the '80s, Whitbread was by far the most characterless.

The last Whitbread pubs to open in Cardiff were the Heritage, on the St Mellons estate, in 1983, and then the Allensbank (now the Grape & Olive) in 1994. The Ely brewery was closed so that Whitbread could switch its brewing operations to a new plant just off the M4 at Magor, which specialised in making lagers like Heineken and Stella Artois. Eventually, Whitbread was itself taken over by Bass-Charrington and sold its Magor operation to a multinational lager-brewer named Interbrew. All the pubs were sold off.

So eventually, after 2000, only Brains was left. They alone had managed to resist being swallowed up, and they were now beginning to expand. Due to a 1997 merger with Crown–Buckley, there is now a Brains presence up the Valleys (which was Crown territory) and in West Wales (the Buckleys brewery was in Llanelli). Brains also has interests in Pembrokeshire, the English Midlands, and other places. They have become a Cardiff success story.

RISE OF THE MICROS

Another success story is Bullmastiff, our local entrant in the 'micro-brewery' stakes.

Brothers Bob and Paul Jenkins opened the Bullmastiff Brewery in Penarth Docks in 1987, brewing award-winning best bitter 'Son of a Bitch'. In 1992 it relocated to Hadfield Road in Leckwith – meaning it just about qualifies for this book.

We should probably also add that Wetherspoons have become a major player on the pub scene in Cardiff, having opened some nine different pubs here since 1999.

Some people knock them, but I like 'em: you can drink proper beer there. Tidy!

Question: The last Ely Ales pub to open was the New Ely (1956). The last Hancocks pub to open was the Master Gunner (1967). The last Whitbread pub to open was the Allensbank (1994). So when was the last new Brains pub to open outside the city centre?

The Pendragon (in Thornhill) opened in 1985, the Canal Boat (now the Blackweir Tavern) in 1990 and Rumpoles (in Adamsdown) in 1991, although it has since closed down. So what is the answer – does anyone out there know?

Okay, enough of pubs and drinking. The other big 'going out' pastime in Victorian and Edwardian Cardiff was going to the music hall. At one time, there were several Cardiff theatres or music halls. By the 1920s, though, these places were beginning to seem a little old-fashioned, due to a new thing called 'the cinema' ...

THE PICTURE PALACES

At one time, there were no less than eight cinemas in the city centre, and twenty-three in the city as a whole. Difficult to believe now, but it's true.

The **Capital** was the biggest in 'town' and on Saturdays there were kids' morning shows ('Saturday matinees'), with science-fiction serials like *Flash Gordon* or *Buck Rogers*, or western heroes like Roy Rogers, Buck Jones and *The Lone Ranger*. A chap (Mr Barker) recently wrote to the *South Wales Echo* recalling his days as a projectionist at the Rialto in Whitchurch. There, kids would bring cap guns to the cowboy films, shooting them at the screen baddies, in between yelling advice like, 'He's behind you!'

The popularity of *The Lone Ranger* was phenomenal. On a Thursday afternoon in 1958, traffic in St Mary Street came to a standstill as thousands of schoolboys packed the area for a quarter of a mile around Howell's department store. The store itself was already rammed, with rows of boys filling staircases and jamming up the aisles. For three hours, there was chaos, until the Lone Ranger himself – played by Clayton Moore, wearing his cowboy hat and black mask – finally turned up. He managed to battle his way through the crowds to get into the store, then made a five-minute appearance: giving an Indian greeting, twirling his six-shooter gun around, then saying goodbye and leaving!

The **Empire** was the next biggest in the city centre and then the **Odeon** and the **Olympia** (later the ABC), which were slightly smaller and almost next door to one another on Queen Street. Another two cinemas showed old films that had already been released and were 'doing the rounds' again. These were the **Queens,** near the corner of Queen Street and Churchill Way, and the **Park Hall,** near the Park Hotel in Park Place.

A seventh cinema in 'town' was the **Central,** which was a local cinema for the residential area on the southern edge of town. This was a fairly dingy area during the 1940s and the rather tatty cinema was known locally as 'the Bug House'. The Central was knocked down in 1959 and an arcade – Oxford Arcade – was built on the site. That arcade has since disappeared with the St David's 2 development. Finally, there was also, at one time, the **Pavilion** in St Mary Street.

Outside 'town', most districts of Cardiff had their own cinema – and some of them had two. For instance, Canton had the **Coliseum** (known as 'the Fleapit') and the **Canton.** The Coliseum was a very basic affair opposite the King's Castle pub, where only a curtain separated the lobby from the auditorium. It was knocked down in the mid-1980s and became the UK's first purpose-built bingo hall. The Canton, the classier of the two cinemas, was turned into a succession of grocery stores – currently it is 'Iceland'.

In Ely, there was the **Regent** on Mill Lane, later knocked down to make way for a nursing home, and the **Avenue**, by the junction of Cowbridge Road and Grand Avenue. This was a relatively plush picture house, which later became a Howell's car salesroom and then a Blockbuster film rental shop.

Other suburban cinemas included the **Ninian** in Penarth Road, Grangetown; the **Tivoli**, now a car showroom, on Station Road, Llandaff North; and the **Rialto** near the Fox and Hounds pub in Whitchurch. Rhiwbina had the **Monico** and Gabalfa had the **Plaza**.

Okay, that covers west and north Cardiff. In central Cardiff, Roath had no less than three cinemas. In City Road, there was the **Gaiety** (later a bingo hall and then a bowling alley), which still stands, now disused, with its eastern-style twin domes. In Albany Road, there was the **Globe**; a music venue now occupies part of the site. And in Clifton Street there was the **Clifton**, which closed down relatively early (1932), becoming a Woolworths and then a Tesco Express.

Cathays had the **Coronet** (another one known as 'the Bughouse') in Woodville Road. Splott had the evocatively named **Splott Cinema** (must've taken 'em a while to dream that one up!) in Agate Street. And east of the River Rumney there was the **County Cinema**, on the corner of Newport Road and Wentloog Road, in Rumney – later knocked down for flats.

So that is some twenty-three cinemas in total. During this golden age of cinema-going (1920–50), there were also five cinemas in Barry and two in Penarth. However, the habit declined badly in the '50s, as more and more people succumbed to the temptation of making a 'picture palace' of their own living room instead, by buying a TV set.

I can just about remember seeing films in the original Capitol, but this closed in 1978, and by the time I was 10, there were just two cinemas in town: the Odeon and the

ABC, almost next door in Queen Street. Outside 'town', a few of the suburban cinemas were hanging on. The Globe tried to operate as a kind of art-house cinema for a while, hoping to attract a student audience. But then in the '70s, the Sherman Theatre opened not so far away, which also showed those kind of films (as well as putting on plays), and the Globe closed in 1981. The building was demolished four years later, but I went to see a band at the Globe lately, and the interior still resembles the interior of a cinema (there is a balcony, for instance, where 'the gods' would have been).

I can also just about remember the Plaza still standing, a disused cinema, on North Road. It had been killed off by the opening of Gabalfa flyover in 1968. The cinema-goers, increasingly car-users, could no longer park nearby and, worse, the sound of all the traffic drowned out the films. The cinema was bulldozed in the mid-'80s and turned into sheltered accommodation.

The last of the suburban cinemas still going after that was the Monico. In my teenage years, this was an interesting alternative to 'going to town'. Kids from my school at Radyr, in the northern outposts of Cardiff, would go there on Saturdays to watch things like *Raiders of the Lost Ark* (1981); it became quite a fad. In the '90s, I went a few times on Saturday nights. They had a decent programme there – you could see *Pulp Fiction* one week and a *Naked Gun* film the next – and it was a more atmospheric venue than the town cinemas, which by that point were turning into multiplexes. The Monico was like an 'old-school' cinema.

Many of the patrons of the Monico in later years were from the Valleys, where most of their own local cinemas had already bitten the dust. So a key factor in finally killing off the Monico – which shut its doors in 2003 – was the opening of the multiplex at Nantgarw, a few miles north of Cardiff. The Monico is now a block of apartments.

This brings us on to the multiplexes. The first one to open in Cardiff was the **Capitol Odeon**, which opened in 1990 near the site of the old Capitol cinema. But this only lasted a few years before the owners, Odeon, decided to switch their operation to the Millennium Plaza, next to the rugby stadium. The *original* Capitol was in the middle of the last block of shops on Queen Street. This was demolished in 1979. The new block was built as part of the 'Capitol Centre' development a decade later, and the multiplex cinema (the Capitol Odeon) was at the eastern end of the block, on the corner with Station Terrace. Two different things, folks!

The coming of the Capitol Odeon, the first multiplex in Cardiff, saw off the last two Queen Street cinemas, the Odeon and the ABC, which soon closed. So now, for the first time since picturehouses came to Cardiff seventy-five years earlier, there was not a single cinema on the entire length of Queen Street (if you take the Capitol Odeon to be on Station Terrace). Instead, shops had taken over, indicating the public's preference for another leisure-time activity called 'shopping'.

Back to the brave new world of the multiplexes. The Capitol Odeon went to the Millennium Plaza and became the Odeon, and the **Cineworld** opened in Mary Ann Street. Also we had the **Vue**, which opened 'down the Bay'. (Mustn't forget the Bay!)

CARDIFF'S NIGHTSPOTS

Before the First World War, the major forms of entertainment when 'going out for the evening' consisted of two things: going to the pub and going to the theatre (or music hall). After the war, two new entertainment forms became popular: the cinema and ballroom dancing. We have just looked at cinema-going. Now we will look at dancing.

Most districts of Cardiff had their dance halls. In Canton, the prime mover in the local dance scene had the unlikely name of Professor Sweeney. The groovy professor opened a dance hall above the Pavlova Billiard Rooms, which was known for years as, simply, the **Pavlova**. (This place is near Tesco's; it is now the Canton Sports Bar.) For years, the Pavlova was one of the places for couples to meet. When my mother was young (in the '40s), she was warned not to go there by her father, who told her it was 'a den of iniquity'. She later discovered that he had first met her mother there!

Down the Victoria Park end of Canton was the **Victoria Ballroom** (later the Victoria Club, now some kind of eaterie), which was a much grander affair than the Pavlova. The smaller places tended to have records played, while the grander ones sometimes had a band – the ladies would wear long dresses and silver shoes.

The craze for dances became so widespread that they could crop up in church halls (often following whist drives), or even school halls. Oddly, during the 1930s, if you finished dancing at the Pavlova (at 11 p.m.), you could carry on at St Luke's church hall, which didn't shut until 1 a.m.

'Dances were generally supposed to be fairly respectable entertainment,' Joan Withers (my mother) recalled. 'In the '40s and '50s, a lot of girls wouldn't go to pubs, because they were not regarded as completely respectable. But they would go to dances.'

Girls would tend to sit on chairs and would be approached by men – who tended to stand – asking them to dance. Dances included, in ascending order of difficulty, the waltz, the paso doble, the quickstep, the foxtrot and the tango (although that was rarely performed).

Girls would often dance with one another, with one 'leading' (the male role). Men would not dance with one another, mind. 'Often a man would ask you to dance, and even if he was not very attractive, you would agree, out of polite-ness. But if he was a good dancer, well, suddenly he did become attractive.'

Bearing this in mind, some men went to dancing school to hone their technique. My uncle Malcolm, for instance, went to the Sylvia & Harry Marks School in Birchgrove.

In 'town', there were Saturday-night dances at the **City Hall**. Again, these were fairly polite affairs – even though there were things like 'the gentlemen's excuse-me', where a random bloke could just cut in, more or less shove a girl's dancing partner out of the way and take over himself. That sort of thing would lead to a punch-up these days, but back in the day, it was just the normal thing.

The City Hall apart, there were bands at the **Gaumont** (formerly the Empire) on Queen Street and in the basement at the **Capitol**. This latter later became the 'Victor Sylvester Dancing School'.

In the early '60s, the Gaumont closed and the basement turned into the **Top Rank Suite** (so called because it was owned by the Rank Organisation). 'The Rank' was initially a ballroom, too. Jack Dorsey's band played there in 1963 and competitive dance contests were also regularly held there. A good local team was the one put out by (the afore-mentioned) Sybil and Harry Marks' School of Dancing, which represented Wales in the BBC TV competition *Come Dancing*. (The Marks' 'School of Dancing' sign could still be seen painted on the window opposite the New Inn pub in Birchgrove until recently. It is now a nursery school.)

By the late '60s, the concept of dance halls was get-ting a bit out-dated for most of the younger generation. They started grooving at places that eventually became known as 'discos', while older punters, looking for some-thing a bit different, began to spend Saturday nights habituating places called 'nightclubs'.

The earliest Cardiff nightclubs were opened by a chap called Annis Abraham. This is not the bloke who writes books about supporting Cardiff City. The chap we are talking about is an older fellow, of the same name, who is the father of the 'Cardiff City Annis'.

Some of Annis' early nightclubs had an Egyptian theme, perhaps in keeping with his Middle Eastern origins. There was the **Sphinx** in Canton – where the Pavlova dance hall used to be – and **Cleopatra's** in Custom House Street.

So Cardiff blinked, wide-eyed, and then staggered into the era of the nightclubs. For a while, the big nightspot in town was **Tito's,** in Greyfriars Road. This was opened by Annis and another local businessman, Gino Rabaiotti. This was, for several years in the 1960s and '70s, a well-known place to see good cabaret acts (upstairs). These included the likes of comedians Bob Monkhouse, Des O'Connor, and singers such as Ronnie Hilton and Tessie O'Shea, plus all-rounders like Roy Castle. Downstairs was a disco.

There has been a nightclub at this venue for many years now, albeit under several different names: since the days of Tito's, it has been Nero's, Coco Savannah's (closed after a fire), Zeus and now whatever-it-is. Oh yeah, Prizm.

In the '60s, as venues began to diversify into youth 'scenes', lovers of soul would tend to go to the **Victoria Club** – formerly the Victoria Ballroom – in Canton on Sunday evenings, where the place became the **Amen Corner**, a soul club. (The band that formed there had the same name.) In the '70s, a groovy soul place was the **Pepperpot** in Womanby Street.

In the late '60s and early '70s, the hippies and rockers began frequenting their own places. There was the **Blue Moon** (or was it just the Moon?) at the top of the Hayes, near Cardiff open market – a great place for rock music – and the **Revolution**, somewhere near the monument at the top of St Mary Street. There were also several places down the docks, but our piece on Butetown in the previous Around the Districts chapter has covered this territory.

Eventually, there were two big discos in town, and a host of other, smaller places, catering for more niche audiences. The two biggies being Tito's, in Greyfriars Road, and the Top Rank Suite – always known as 'the Rank' – in Queen Street.

In the '90s, the Rank went through a bewildering number of name changes, including Panama Joe's, the Astoria and others, before eventually conking out altogether. There is no nightclub there now, just a Primark clothes store. Sad, in a way, as it meant that another crucial piece of Cardiff history 'bit the dust'.

At this point David has piped up. He wants to tell us about his …

TOP TEN NIGHTS OUT IN CARDIFF

1. The Top Rank
The only place to start. Less a nightclub, more a rite of passage. Like a time capsule buried beneath the modern HMV, this enormous giant cellar, was, quite frankly, Shangri-La.

My early visits came around 1969. Amazingly, in those days the Rank used to open its doors to 11-year-olds on Saturday mornings. And so I was introduced at this tender age to Ashton, Gardner & Dyke's Resurrection Shuffle, soulful tunes from The Temptations, and other wonders of Tamla Motown. These dark tunes from Detroit and Philadelphia seemed entirely at home in this giant, imposing cavern, and, like most of the rest of the city's youth, I spent many happy nights over the coming years under its enormous balcony, pretending to be Starsky … or Hutch.

2. The Cavern

Just around the corner from the Rank, in Crockherbtown Lane, stood the Cavern.

One or two notches down the food chain from the Rank perhaps but, as my adolescence developed into my teens, this was to prove a popular and successful little addition to my social calendar. This was the era of Hot Chocolate and Barry White, and I was having a ball. It always seemed like this venue had a more relaxed take on the 18s-and-over rule, as many a spotty teen managed to sneak in on a Saturday night. And if you were one, do you recall the free burger and peas that came with the price of entry? Sure you do!

Fashion was something of a free-for-all at the Cavern, as the glam-rock era did its best to keep up with the New Wave. I still recall one almighty mistake, as a girlfriend and I once turned up wearing black cap-sleeve T-shirts, black bottoms and matching thin red belts. Who needs Rod and Britt, eh?

3. Tito's

Ah, doing it for real now. One of the few venues in this list that actually still exists. These days it is called Pryzm and over the years it has gone by various names – Kon Tikki, Oceana – But to many, that magical-looking parlour opposite the New Theatre on Greyfriars Road will always be Tito's.

The joint was about as '70s as it gets. Flares and wide collars, a cabaret room upstairs, and half-price beer before 10 p.m. on a Sunday, this was a place to fall in and out of love in. And we all did.

4. Bakers Row

Now I know I was an impressionable age, but I was always quite impressed by Bakers Row. It seemed to possess an air of sophistication beyond that of other venues. Was it

*because the '80s were coming? Was it the Roxy Music
soundtrack? Or its proximity to Howell's department store
in swanky little Wharton Street? Or was I just growing up
a bit? It was time to dress up when you hit Bakers Row.
I always enjoyed my evenings there.*

5. The Moon
*If Bakers Row and Tito's were home to the Fashion Police,
then this place was most definitely off their beat.*

*Never a place I frequented a great deal to be honest,
the heavy rock music, imposing atmosphere and scattered
bottles of Newcy Brown being, well, just not my cup of tea
I suppose. There will always be a demand for places like this.
(The Revolution was a similar rock-based venue, as I recall.)
No dress code to speak of, and lots of standing and milling
around. For some reason, I also recall an enormous, iron
fire-escape-type staircase.*

*The Moon stood somewhere around Mill Lane, maybe
near the current John Lewis, which is about as far away from
The Moon as it is possible to get!*

6. The Mont Merence
*Another venue with something of a relaxed dress code,
this wonderful club – one of many colourful fun spots
on Charles Street – sadly also no longer exists. 'Monties'
catered essentially for the student audience, but also proved
just as popular with the locals. Officially it was a 'members
only' joint, though I am sure I once gained entry by flashing
a Cardiff City Supporters Club card. My visits took places
during the early '80s. I have especially fond memories of the
1981 Christmas party, for example, with the Human League
to dance to. 'Monties' would be many people's choice for
the best club ever. They could well be right.*

7. The Dowlais
Like no other place on earth.

The Dowlais sat on West Bute Street, accessed via a shadowy lane and narrow doorway.

Inside, it was just like the Tardis. The place seemed much larger than it could possibly be from the outside. There were two bars downstairs and a stage where the top pub acts of the day would make Friday night down the docks a real party.

The local band scene was thriving back then, and names like Red Beans and Rice, the Spasm Band, Young Marble Giants, Snatch It Back, Moira and the Mice, Laverne Brown, The Frames, and Boys Have Emotions were all there or thereabouts. Splott-based Razzam once supported The Domino's at the nearby Casablanca, featuring local boy Pino Palladino on bass, later to become bassist for Paul Young, and eventually for The Who.

Back at the Dowlais, Fire Down Below, Whisper Zone, Denim and even Racing Cars (1970s one-hit wonder merchants from the Rhondda) are some of the names I remember from these great days. Upstairs, Smugglers Disco drew me further in.

Down the docks. Heaven.

8. The Claude
The Claude is another of the few venues described here that is still going. An enormous barn of a place located on the corner of Albany Road near Claude Road in Roath, the establishment is, quite honestly, all things to all men. I have been going to the Claude for over thirty years, yet remarkably I have always felt at home there. The clientele have all aged alongside me, while new young blood has been effortlessly absorbed. Probably catering for a similar client base as the old Dowlais, it is home to all. A strong student customer base

is supplemented by grisly Cardiff drinkers, gangs of women dolled up for a night out, stag nights, live bands, real ale, food, a beer garden and a 3D TV for when the football is on. Its location, in the heart of 'Student land', places it handily for the fast-food market, while more discerning diners can grab a post-pint meal at a range of hospitable eateries, such as the long-established Tandoori Mahal.

The Claude is, quite simply, great. Frankly I am never quite sure why I drink anywhere else.

9. The Wynford

'Your Honour, I swear that I have never set foot in the venue.'

'Really? Are you really asking the court to accept your story that, on the night in question, you were nowhere near this charming city-centre hotel on Clare Street, just yards from the Millennium Stadium, with its reputation for noisy nights and friendly welcomes from middle-aged women ... Is that really what you are telling us?!'

'Get me my lawyer ...'

10. Miss Jones

And so my odyssey comes almost bang up to date.

This is one of the newer venues in the city, nestling in the leafy suburb of Whitchurch, on Merthyr Road.

Miss Jones seems to have glanced through the above list, ticking off all the key ingredients to deliver the perfect modern Cardiff night out. Officially described as a 'Cocktail Lounge and Restaurant', maybe it caters more for my middle-aged self rather than that skinny youth who blagged his way into Tito's as a 16-year-old, but the place works. Squeeze into your 'pulling shirt' with your mates on a busy Saturday, grab your cowboy hat to dance away a Girls Nite Out, or cwtch up in a cosy corner for that romantic dish of tapas.

*It's easy to find, free to enter and fun for all. It shines out
as an example of the sophisticated capital, yet still retains
that feeling of 'Cardiffness' that characterises all of the
venues I have talked about above.*

Taxi for Collins ...?

AND THE BAND PLAYED ON

When rock 'n' roll hit Cardiff in the late 1950s, the Capitol
Theatre was still essentially a cinema, rather than a con-
cert venue. The early rockers played at places like the **New
Theatre** (for instance, Marty Wilde) and the **Gaumont
Theatre**, a cinema in Queen Street.

In the early '60s, the package tours came in, with many
groups and artists touring together. A typical programme
at the Gaumont in this era had American rocker Conway
Twitty supported by Freddy Cannon (of 'Running Bear'
fame), Johnny Preston, ginger British rocker Wee Willie
Harris and The Cannonballs, plus Tony Crombie and Chris
Wayne & the Echoes. Now that is a full programme!

The **Capitol** took off as a concert venue after the Rank
Organisation bought it in 1964. Over the next decade, nearly
all of the top British acts played there. The Beatles featured
there three times, including the last two nights of what
turned out to be their final British tour, in December 1965.
They undertook a final US tour the following year, but
The Beatles were last seen by fans in Britain – apart
from a rooftop gig in London in 1969 – playing at the
Capitol. Amazing!

Another noteworthy event at the Capitol was the famous
Kinks bust-up in 1965, when guitarist Dave Davies was
involved in an onstage punch-up with drummer Mick Avory.
These shenanigans contributed to the group not being able
to get a visa to tour the USA for four years in the late '60s.

Also featured at the Capitol in this decade were Bob Dylan, The Rolling Stones, The Small Faces and The Hollies (these latter two groups played a double-header in 1966). The Beach Boys played there twice as well.

The '70s kicked in and the Capitol continued to be one of the country's prime concert venues. Cardiff audiences were able to see chart-topping pop stars like T Rex, Slade and David Essex. For the slightly older and more discerning 'rock' crowd there were the likes of Led Zeppelin, Deep Purple and Black Sabbath, plus Hawkwind, Uriah Heep, Wishbone Ash and Status Quo. What about that weird thing with big keyboards and funny hats – what was it called? Ah yes, 'prog-rock'. Well, there was also ELP, Yes (twice) and Peter Gabriel.

From the USA came Lynyrd Skynyrd and Ted Nugent, and from Germany, pioneering electro-poppers Kraftwerk. Later gigs included Supertramp, Rainbow, Rod Stewart and Elton John; the last major gig was possibly Thin Lizzy in December 1977. The venue closed and was knocked down in 1979. Shame.

The closure of the Capitol was arguably a blow from which Cardiff has never recovered. Other venues tried to fill the gap for a while – notably the **Top Rank**, previously better known as a disco, further along Queen Street. The Rank began hosting gigs in the early '70s: folk-rockers Lindisfarne played there in 1972, supported by Genesis. The heyday of the Rank as a live venue, though, was just about to come, with a number of top punk banks playing there, including The Clash, Siouxsie and the Banshees, X-Ray Spex, The Boomtown Rats, The Lurkers and The Rich Kids.

Sophia Gardens Pavilion had an interesting history. It opened in 1951 as part of the UK-wide Festival of Britain, and was supposed to be Cardiff's version of the Earls Court arena in London, hosting Ideal Home exhibitions, dog shows and corporate get-togethers.

The Pavilion occasionally, over the years, sprang to life as a concert venue. American comic Danny Kaye had headlined there as early as 1952 – although this was hardly rock 'n' roll! Pink Floyd, the kings of prog-rock, do not appear to have played the Capitol, but they certainly played the Pavilion, possibly on more than one occasion. They played there in 1967 as part of a package tour headlined by The Move, and which also featured The Jimi Hendrix Experience, The Nice and local favourites Amen Corner. In January 1982 the roof collapsed and that was that! Where the Pavilion once stood is now a car park.

However, Cardiff City Council was about to open its St David's Centre shopping mall, and contained within the development was a new concert venue – **St David's Hall**. St David's became a decent venue for seeing '60s revival package tours and occasional niche artists, from John Cale to Kirsty McColl, as well as classical players like Nigel Kennedy; however, the big-name bands were lacking throughout the '80s and there seemed to be a complete vacuum for major gigs in Cardiff.

My recollections are backed up, to some extent, by Dave Owens, the music editor of the *South Wales Echo* (who is roughly my age). Dave mentioned his first gig being The Jam in 1982 – not in Cardiff, but at Shepton Mallet Show Pavilion in Somerset. This place was basically a cattle market and, for a while, this seemed to be the closest that anyone 'big' got to play in Cardiff.

Of course, the problem was that bands – and more importantly, promoters and managers – wanted to play bigger venues. The Capitol was a 3,000-seater venue and St David's Hall was 2,000, but by the '80s this was not really big enough to get itself a slot on most bands' UK tours.

The need for a bigger venue was finally resolved by the opening of the 7,000-capacity **Cardiff International Arena** (known as 'the CIA') in 1993. Many big name acts now come to Cardiff to play here (although it is now officially the 'Motorpoint Arena').

That just about covers performers who have come to Cardiff to play gigs. But what about famous performers from Cardiff?

SHIRLEY BASSEY:
THE GIRL FROM ... SPLOTT

Wales is famous for its singers. Not all of the famous Welsh singers are from Cardiff, of course, but some of them are ...

The first name that springs to mind is Shirley Bassey. She made it big on the West End stage in the late 1950s and won worldwide fame during the years that followed, not least for her renditions of two of the best James Bond theme songs: *Goldfinger* (1964) and *Diamonds Are Forever* (1971). She was the first singer to be asked to sing a Bond theme a second time; in 1979, she completed a hat-trick with *Moonraker* (1979).

Shirley, who was born in Cardiff of a Yorkshire mother and a Nigerian sailor father, came to be seen by many as a typical product of 'Tiger Bay', Cardiff's famous/infamous Docks area. This 'Tiger Bay' heritage was frequently used in promoting her career from the early days, since the area seemed to evoke a certain exotic romanticism. The association of Shirley with Tiger Bay has continued to this day, with the Manic Street Preachers (who are Valleys boys from Blackwood) writing 'The Girl from Tiger Bay' for her just a few years back. But to those Cardiffians 'in the know', there is an urban myth at work here, for (whisper it softly) **Shirley Bassey is not from Tiger Bay**. Not really ...

Shirley grew up in the 1930s in Portmanmoor Road in the somewhat less romantic-sounding environs of **Splott**. She only spent her very early years in the docks; her formative years were spent very much in Splott, where she attended Moorland Road School. Yet this is rarely mentioned, and probably nobody outside Cardiff ever associates Shirley Bassey with Splott. Perhaps few people outside Cardiff have ever heard of Splott. This is fine, except that it frequently drives the old-time residents of Splott nuts!

So, you heard it here first (or – if you are from Splott – you didn't): **Shirley Bassey, the Girl from Splott**. No, it doesn't sound the same, does it!

Shirley is, these days, an international star, with a reputation that is almost untouchable. But people weren't always queueing up to hear her sing – far from it! As a teenage girl, **she simply could not stop singing**, despite frequent pleas to her to desist from doing so. Just after the war, one of the local steelworks, Currans, organised an annual train trip to London, and there are recurring stories that, during these journeys, Shirley was frequently told to shut up. These remonstrations didn't seem to stop her, though, and on she went. And on, and on, and on …

Of course, Shirley had the last laugh. Eventually people were paying a lot of money to hear her sing. And still are, in fact.

WHOLE LOTTA SHAKIN' GOING ON

Despite the glamorous names available to pop fans through-
out the 1980s – Duran Duran, George Michael or even
Frankie Goes to Hollywood – one of the biggest-selling art-
ists of those times was an Ely boy. Our Shaky.

Michael Barratt had been born in Cardiff in 1948 – one
of thirteen children. He adopted the stage name Shakin'
Stevens, but his musical career looked destined for the local
pub scene, as his group 'Shakin' Stevens & the Sunsets'
failed to really make it, despite various record deals and
occasional appearances on national TV shows such as
The Geordie Scene *(in 1974).*

But fame was about to come calling. Shaky's leg-trem-
bling dance moves, '50s hairstyle and Elvis-style vocals led
to his big break when he played the title role in the stage
show Elvis! *in the late '70s. There was no looking back after*
that, and throughout the '80s, Shaky boasted a string of hits,
based loosely on an Elvis-tribute style which appealed to all
generations. My niece is almost 40 now, but she still remi-
nisces longingly of her first-ever concert: Shakin' Stevens at
Newport Centre on St David's Day 1987.

Shaky hit the number one spot in 1981 with a rock 'n' roll
remake of 'This Ole House' (recorded by Rosemary Clooney
in 1954), and again later the same year with the old Frankie
Vaughan hit 'Green Door'. He topped the chart again in 1985,
grabbing the much sought-after Christmas number one spot
with the evergreen 'Merry Christmas Everyone'.

By 1985, Shaky was the best-selling British chart artist
of the decade, with eighteen Top 20 hits. He ended the
'80s behind only Madonna in UK singles sales – beating
Queen, Cliff Richard, U2 and, yes, even Michael Jackson.
In all, Shaky has recorded an amazing thirty-three UK
Top 40 singles.

Inevitably perhaps, the '90s saw the hits dry up, and Shaky retreated from the scene a little. Recent times have seen a bit of a resurgence, though, including a thirtieth anniversary tour in 2011. There is even a Shaky calendar available for 2015. I just know that my niece has bought one.

A BROAD (CALLED) CHURCH

Quite where Charlotte Church sits on the register of all-time Cardiff greats is hard to determine.

Had this book been published a decade ago, then there is little doubt that her star would have been seen high in the city's firmament. Her first album – Voice of an Angel, released in 1998 – included arias, traditional and sacred songs that sold heavily, making her the youngest name with a number one album on the British classical crossover charts.

Her big break came at the tender age of 11, when she sang Andrew Lloyd Webber's 'Pie Jesu' over the telephone on the TV show This Morning in 1997. This was followed soon after by her performance on ITV's Big, Big Talent Show. These appearances rapidly led to concerts at huge venues like Cardiff Arms Park and the Royal Albert Hall; she even opened for Shirley Bassey in Antwerp.

Charlotte was never quite part of that whole 'Cool Cymru' thing – that was a label that became tied around Catatonia, the Manic Street Preachers and others – but she was certainly something to shout about.

In 2005, she issued her first pop album Tissues and Issues, and enjoyed a degree of success in the pop singles chart. Lasting success in this field never quite came to her, though, and, for a while, Charlotte's 'off the field' antics earned her almost as much news print as her performances in the recording studio. Her relationship with one of the rising stars of Welsh rugby, Gavin Henson, looked like a match made in Heaven for the girl with the 'voice of an angel', as the press gleefully elevated the young couple into a Welsh 'Posh and Becks'.

The 'posh' tag never quite sat that easily with 'Charlie Church', though. Despite her Howells School education, she still came across, in her frequent media appearances, as much more of a down-to-earth 'chips in Caroline Street' kinda girl.

She was certainly a proper national celebrity – by which I mean not just in Wales. She was immortalised by Catherine Tate, whose foul-mouthed 'Gran' character once famously described her in a Christmas special as 'Voice of an Angel, Liver of a Wino'. Charlotte, who was making a cameo appearance in the show, went along well with the joke, but it seemed to sum up the demons that began to surround the no-longer-childlike songstress. Gavin and Charlotte ceased to be an item in 2010.

Our girl has been no stranger to controversy and has endured media interest over her fluctuating weight, her smoking and her drinking. But instead of issuing timid apologies or halting explanations, she always stands her ground. 'Generally for me, slimness comes with a little bit of upset or stress … I'd rather be fat and happy, to be honest,' she said in 2010.

Reputed to be worth £25 million in 2003, by 2010 she was down to £11 million, according to the Sunday Times 'Rich List'. The mother-of-two told Stylist magazine, 'I haven't got a lot of money. I've got enough to be comfortable if I was reasonable for the rest of my life, but I'm not reasonable – so I will have to find another way to sustain my lifestyle.'

In the summer of 2006, she began work on her own TV programme, The Charlotte Church Show. After a pilot episode, which caused some controversy and which was never released to the public, the Channel 4 series began in September 2006. The show, which featured two celebrity guests each week, involved music, sketches, reality TV, interviews … and some very colourful language. At one *point, it averaged 1.9 million viewers (10 per cent of the available audience). She also sat in for Zoë Ball on Radio 2's Saturday breakfast show in September 2011.*

In 2012, Charlotte Church appeared on Question Time, *when she backed the findings of the Leveson Inquiry – calling it a 'real and practical way of dealing with the problems of the press'. The former child star, herself a victim of press intrusion, spoke eloquently and with conviction, arguing the case for tough press regulation, and clashing with former* News of the World *executive editor Neil Wallis. You don't take this girl on lightly!*

Charlotte continues to redefine herself at every opportunity. She recently featured in an all-star TV version of Under Milk Wood. *The year 2014 saw her perform at the Dinefwr Literature Festival with an eclectic set of pop, funk and soul. The festival also featured her in conversation with Kat Banyard, discussing … feminist activism. You can always expect the unexpected with this one.*

Quite where Charlotte Church goes next is, frankly, anyone's guess. As a child, she was one of the world's most famous sopranos. As a teenager, she sold millions of records and made a fortune. She performed for the Pope, President Clinton, the Queen, Jay Leno and David Letterman. She has even sung with Luciano Pavarotti. And, of course, she has won – lest we forget – the 'Rear of the Year' competition. So there is plenty of good stuff behind her.

Where will she go next? She might write a historical novel, launch her own bohemian music festival or enter the Eurovision Song Contest. She may appear on Newsnight *one night and be sat next to you, in your local curry house, the next. She has seen the highs and lows of celebrity status, and keeps coming out intact at the other end. With Charlotte, it seems, we just don't know quite what to expect. A broad church, indeed.*

CAN I BE FRANK?

Many towns in the 1970s produced their own local folk singers-cum-comics. Birmingham had Jasper Carrott, Mike Harding was the Rochdale Cowboy, Billy Connolly was the Big Yin fae Glasgow, the West Country had The Wurzels and Cornwall had Jethro.

I guess the nearest thing in Cardiff to such a figure would be Frank Hennessy.

In many ways, Frank is about as 'Kaairdiff' as you can get. He comes from good Cardiff-Irish stock and his speech is littered with rasping vowels and colloquialisms. Listening to Frank singing – and telling jokes in between the songs – is the aural equivalent of eating cockles from Cardiff market, or reading an Echo *column with Dan O'Neill mistily recalling something-or-other.*

I first became aware of Frank in the late 1960s. Back then he was a member of a lively folk combo called The Hennessys. The band also featured Frank's long-time musical partner Dave Burns. This gig, though, was not held in some smoky

Brains pub or dimly lit folk club. Rather, The Hennessys per-
formed live at Moorland Road Junior School, in the heart of
Splott, to an excited and scruffy young audience. I was about
10 years old. That memory has always stayed with me. I think
it was the first group I ever saw play live.

Over the years, Frank went on to make a name for himself on the 'poems and pints' circuit, spinning light-hearted
tales and ditties about life in the capital's long dark streets.
His Cardiff Born, Cardiff Bred *anthem includes lines that*
have taken their own place in the local vocabulary. He is
also a respected authority on the folk scene, appearing
regularly as a host on Radio Wales with his show Celtic
Heartbeat. *He has created and presented TV programmes,*
including Frank Hennessy's Ireland *(2000);* Way Out West
(1998), which explored the roots of Cajun, Cape Breton
and Appalachian music; and Way Down Under, *which*
examined the music and culture of Australia from a Celtic
perspective. As far as 'folk' is concerned, Frank does really
'know his onions'.

And for many Cardiffians, Frank retains a special place
in their hearts. Indeed, there would have been several raised
eyebrows had he not featured somewhere in the pages of
this book.

Of course, it could be said that Frank no longer represents a Cardiff that still exists. His wittily titled album,
Cardiff After Dark, *is a typical demonstration of his art. But*
who actually drinks Brains Dark these days? Surely in the
modern estate pubs of Pentrebane, Pentwyn or Gabalfa, it's
more likely to be 'Kairdiff After Karlsberg'? Okay, there is
no pun in that phrase, but you get the point. Still, it's good
to be reminded of Cardiff traditions and there's no disput-
ing that Frank belongs firmly within these pages.

HENNESSY:
COGNAC FOR THE CARDIFFIANS

I saw Frank perform for the first time about eight years ago. He was playing with The Hennessys at The Point – the perfect small, smoky club venue for his brand of entertainment. He has developed a comfortable and easy stage presence over the years, the jokes and anecdotes meshing perfectly with songs about Cardiff, Wales and places further afield. People sang along to stuff they recognised about the 'Grangetown Whale' and 'Billy the Seal'. But they were also moved by the performances of folk standards, which Frank and his band are also adept at playing. In my book, he is a very skilled performer.

Frank also said something very interesting that night. Now, Dan O'Neill has mentioned his (Dan's) Cardiff-Irish background and how that makes him cheer for Ireland at rugby and celebrate St Patrick's Day with gusto.

Although there is a drop of Paddy in me, I am not of a strong Cardiff-Irish background – I am 'Cardiff Wenglish' more than anything – and I feel no particular affinity for Ireland. Dan's cheering for Ireland (even when they play Wales!) at rugby just makes me shake my head in bafflement.

Anyway, Frank said this: 'When I was in my teens, growing up in Cardiff, I felt I was Irish. Then I went to Ireland and realised I was Welsh. I also realised that it was just as interesting to be Welsh as it was to be Irish.' These are wise words indeed.

Of Frank's stories, how much is true and how much is mythology? Well, 'Billy the Seal' is true – there was a seal living in the pond at Victoria Park for many years – whereas the 'Grangetown Whale' is pure comic invention. But we are all slightly mythologising Cardiff, are we not?

For instance, there is a TV channel now broadcasting (*Made in Cardiff*), which features a programme called

What's Occurring, Cardiff? Nobody in Cardiff ever said 'what's occurring' before the character of Nessa (who is actually supposed to be from Barry, not Cardiff) was created for a comedy show called *Gavin and Stacey*. No doubt this phrase may well become a commonly used Cardiff saying in years to come. Or maybe it won't. But the point is, it is not authentic Cardiff – it is made up. The first time I heard the phrase 'what's occurring?' on TV was when David Jason said it, in an episode of *Inspector Frost*. That was about twenty years ago, and it was set in the Thames Valley – nowhere near Cardiff.

Likewise, there are the geezers who run 'the Diff' website. Nobody ever called Cardiff 'the Diff' before they came along. Their nickname may also catch on. And what about the *South Wales Echo* and their reports on a cricket team in Cardiff, which they mysteriously insist on calling 'Glammy'? When did you ever hear a real person call Glamorgan 'Glammy' for Pete's sake?

But then, I think back twenty years to when a guy called Phil Stead was running around the away terrace at Cardiff City games, slapping his head like a maniac. Eventually, everyone joined in, and 'doing the Ayatollah' was born. Now it is part of Cardiff culture, in the same way that Frank Hennessy's phrases have become part of the culture. All 'culture' has to start somewhere.

Put frankly, Frank Hennessy is well and truly part of Cardiff's folk culture. Long may he remain so. Truly, Hennessy is cognac for the Cardiff masses.

TARZAN WAS NEARLY FROM CARDIFF

Tarzan could have been from Cardiff.

Billy Kimber was from Pomeroy Street in Butetown and was a keen sportsman. He had learned to swim at the age of 4 by taking a dip in the nearby Glamorganshire Canal. During the First World War, he became heavyweight boxing champion of the Royal Engineers. After the war, he was a Welsh champion swimmer, as well as playing at forward for Cardiff Athletic and Penarth. His day job was running his own ship's chandlery business down Cardiff Docks – but even in business hours, he was wont to dive into Tiger Bay from the mast of a ship and then swim underneath the mighty vessel, before emerging on the other side.

Word spread of Billy's fantastic aquatic feats, and in the 1930s, when MGM were trying to find a strong swimmer to portray Tarzan in a series of films, Billy's name was put forward by a London casting agency. Billy was invited to London for an audition, but he was too busy running his business. Johnny Weissmuller (an Olympic swimming champion from Germany) ended up getting the part instead. Johnny wasn't bad, but Billy would have been better!

7

CARDIFF –
WHERE'S 'AT, AGAIN?

We began this book with a chapter that explored the geographical location of Cardiff and the historical evolution of the city. Now we will have a quick closing look on where Cardiff stands culturally.

First of all, David – who is a keen Welsh learner – gives us an insight into the use of the Welsh language in the city. I take issue with a number of David's points here – I wanted to scribble all over what he had written but he wouldn't let me – and there is not room in this book for two separate pieces!

And remember, please, I am not taking issue with all of his points – just some of them. I wrote about the history of the Celts in Chapter 1, so I am well aware that the Welsh language was 'here first'. Long may it thrive.

WELSH IN THE CITY

Whilst Cardiff's pride in its 'Welshness' is often proclaimed, attitudes to the Welsh language in the capital vary.

Despite roaring out 'O bydded yr hen iaith barhau' ('O long may the old language continue') each time the anthem is sung, many Cardiffians are ambivalent – or even downright hostile – towards the old Celtic tongue.

The reasons for this are a little complicated. Welsh may once have been the language of the common people of Wales, but then Cardiff – and the South Wales Valleys – experienced the Industrial Revolution and Welsh was obliterated by English as the language of the new migrant industrial working class.

In recent years, Welsh has made a comeback in Cardiff, but it is hardly the language of 'the common people' anymore. Rather, it has come to be associated with middle-class media types who work for public-funded organisations such as BBC Wales, S4C or the Welsh Assembly.

In addition, many 'ordinary' Cardiffians resent the fact that the Welsh-language lobby has forced the Assembly to plough millions into bilingual signs, documents and translation services – all to prop up a 'dead language' that hardly anyone in the city speaks or uses, or so the argument runs.

Oh, we know there are pockets of Welsh speakers in Pontcanna and Llandaff, but is it really worth printing everything twice for a handful of activists? Do we really need the road signs to direct us to 'Y Sblot' (Splott) or even 'Bae Caerdydd' (Cardiff Bay)?

Before the Industrial Revolution, Welsh was the dominant language when Cardiff was but a small town huddled around the castle. First-language Welsh speakers became the minority from the 1820s onwards, as the town rapidly expanded. At work, as many found themselves interacting with English, Irish and Scottish migrants, the use of English began to predominate. For the native Cardiffians, Welsh remained the language of home and chapel, and it was during this period that most Welsh chapels and churches were established. But within a generation, many of these chapels had become English-speaking. The First World War was probably the final nail in the coffin, as English became the language of choice for state communication.

In recent years, the process of industrialisation, immigration and dilution of the Welsh language has been reversed a little. As Cardiff has expanded as an administrative capital of Wales in the last sixty years, many first-language Welsh speakers have migrated here from other parts of Wales. This has increased social activities in Welsh.

Welsh speakers all over Wales guard the language fiercely, and Cardiff is no exception. Tŷ'r Cymru (House of Wales) was established in 1936 as a centre for Welsh speakers to meet socially. The Urdd Centre in Pontcanna became another focal point. Y Dinesydd (The Citizen) *began in 1973 and is the oldest Welsh-language newspaper for Cardiff residents. Its pages today are full of reports of Welsh-language activities in the city.*

Menter Caerdydd (Cardiff Enterprise) was established in 1998 with the aim of promoting and extending the use of the Welsh-language in the city. Menter offers activities such as weekly clubs for children and young people and school holiday care schemes and social activities for Welsh learners.

How many Welsh speakers are there in Cardiff, then? Well, in 1951, this figure stood at 9,600. By 1991, this had almost doubled to 17,000, and then doubled again to exceed 36,000 by the 2011 census.

Of course, almost anything can be proved with statistics, and saying 'nos da' to the kids at night doesn't make you 'fluent Welsh'. But certainly, things have changed in Cardiff. Broadcaster Vaughan Roderick, for example, describes how he lives 'in an area of Cardiff where Welsh can be heard every day in the park, and half the children are in Welsh-language primary schools. Cardiff is a very different place now to when I was growing up.'

Vaughan mentions education. In 1990, Welsh became a compulsory subject for all students up to the age of 14 in Wales; by 1999, it became compulsory up to the age of 16. But the number of parents choosing Welsh education for their children has had a huge impact on the increase of

Welsh speakers in Cardiff. In 2000–09 for example, seven new Welsh schools were opened in the city. And it's not just in the affluent, middle-class suburbs, either – there is growing demand for Welsh in Leckwith, Canton and Riverside, too. A new high school, Ysgol Bro Edern, has been established on Llanedeyrn Road, whilst a strong parental support group 'RhAG' operates out of Cardiff Gate Business Park. At Ysgol Y Berllan Deg, on the edge of Llanedeyrn, 84 per cent of pupils come from non-Welsh-speaking homes.

In total, there are currently seventeen Welsh-language primary schools and three secondary schools across the city, and an increasing number of opportunities for children to use the language outside of school.

The increasing popularity and use of the language provides opportunities across the social and cultural life of the city. Cardiff has hosted the National Eisteddfod and the Urdd Eisteddfod, which is primarily aimed at young people. Cardiff also hosts its own Welsh-language festival, featuring live music, literature, art, food and drink, sports, comedy, drama and activities for families. Tafwyl is an annual festival established in 2006 to celebrate the use of the Welsh language in Cardiff. Today the festival is part of the Cardiff Festival and in 2012 attracted over 10,000 people, with the main event taking place at Cardiff Castle.

Recently, Clwb Ifor Bach, the focal point of Welsh music in Cardiff, celebrated its 30th birthday. The club opened on Womanby Street in 1983. Originally it was a club for members only, known as 'the Welsh club', but increasingly it attracted artists and bands from across Wales to perform there. Radio 1 DJ Huw Stephens said: 'Since opening, Clwb Ifor Bach has been central to Welsh music in Cardiff and South Wales. The list of Welsh and international bands that have performed there is extensive, and the atmosphere is always exciting.'

There is also a thriving Welsh-language rugby scene in Cardiff. So, far from being a dead tongue, the old language is most definitely alive and kicking in the old city. Whether you think the amount of public spending is justified though, well, that is down to you I guess.

ST DAVID'S DAY PARADE

Despite a degree of popular support, there is currently no official holiday in Wales on 1 March – St David's Day.

The feast day of David (c. 540–c. 600) is the oldest continuously celebrated saint's day in the world, having been observed in Wales since 800.

Cardiff's civic leaders failed to mark the day in any official capacity for years, until 2004. Each year since then, it has grown in size and significance, with more and more Cardiffians booking the day off work. The parade and pageant through the streets has evolved into a joyous, anarchic display of the range of Welsh possibilities. Local schools and many other organisations now assemble in King Edward VII Avenue to snake their way through the city-centre streets.

Despite being an officially sanctioned event, it still has something of a 'home-made' feel to it, with gaily coloured costumes accompanying a forest of St David's Cross flags as the city once again displays it Welshness.

When I was at junior school, we always had an Eisteddfod on St David's Day and a half-day. I don't know why we can't have an official half-day off for St David's Day in Wales. Brains and Wetherspoons could offer special Welsh cuisine, and it would go down a treat, I am sure. If we always did it on the first Friday after 1 March, there would be no problem of absenteeism from work the following day.

NEVER MIND THE BALLOTS!

Commons People

Cardiff has four seats in the UK Parliament at Westminster – or, rather, three and a half. These are: Cardiff West, Cardiff North, Cardiff Central, Cardiff South and Penarth. Penarth, of course, is outside Cardiff, in the Vale of Glamorgan – hence the 'half-a-seat'.

The **Cardiff South and Penarth** seat has been called various things in the past, such as Cardiff South and Cardiff South-East. Penarth was thrown in with it in 1983, and now it also contains Sully. Since 1945, it has always been represented by a Labour MP. On the face of it, this would seem to make it a 'safe Labour' seat. In fact, though, it has sometimes been very marginal; in recent elections, the margin of victory has only tended to be a few thousand votes.

There have been three Labour MPs since the war. **Jim Callaghan**, a native of Portsmouth, held it from 1945–87. It has been claimed that he was originally selected to fight the seat because he had an Irish name, and it would be assumed by the many Irish-descended steelworkers and dockers of Cardiff South that he was 'one of us'. Callaghan proved to be quite an astute politician, working his way through the Labour ranks to eventually become Prime Minister (1976–79).

'Sunny Jim' has the unique distinction of being the only politician ever to hold all four traditional 'great offices of state': Prime Minister, Chancellor of the Exchequer, Foreign Secretary and Home Secretary. He continued in the Commons for some time after he was PM, and eventually also became 'Father of the House' (longest continuously serving MP). Finally, he stood down from the Commons and went to the Lords. He died in 2005.

'Sunny Jim' was succeeded as MP by **Alun Michael**, a North Walian (from Anglesey) who had developed close ties with Cardiff, having been a reporter for the *Echo*, a city councillor and manager of a boys' home in Ely, before becoming MP. He was a hard-working MP who won favour with Tony Blair, and was a Home Office minister before allowing the PM to talk him into entering Welsh Assembly politics.

After a brief period as leader of the Welsh Assembly Government, Alun returned to Westminster politics (he was still the MP for Cardiff South) and became an Environment Minister. He left Westminster in 2012 for the important-sounding role of Police and Crime Commissioner for South Wales – a job he took on at the age of 69.

When Alun became the police commissioner, he was followed in the Westminster seat by **Stephen Doughty**, another Labourite (born in Llandaff, raised in Llantwit Major). The majority at the last two elections has been between 4,000 and 6,000 – meaning that the seat has become decidedly marginal. However, we have been here before.

In 1959, Jim Callaghan – then a leading Labour 'shadow minister' – only held on by a few hundred votes. This led the Tories to mount a full-scale assault on the seat in 1964 with someone they thought was a sure-fire 'hit' candidate: recent England Test cricket captain Ted Dexter. Unfortunately for the Tories, though, the tough dockers and steelworkers were not overly impressed by a toff (his nickname was 'Lord Ted') and refused to believe that he had any idea about politics. Callaghan got back in with a majority that had increased seven-fold. Lord Ted went back to the world of cricket.

The other Cardiff seat that has usually been 'safe Labour' is **Cardiff West. George Thomas**, a tremendously effective constituency MP, held the seat from 1945 until his retirement in 1983. The much-loved George was Welsh Secretary from 1968–70 (in the Wilson government), and then Speaker of the Commons from 1976–83.

During his tenure as Mr Speaker, the BBC managed to persuade the Commons to allow radio broadcasts of debates. Prior to the first broadcast, a producer from 'the Beeb' told George that they needed him calling 'Order' as the introduction to their radio show – he would need to say it quite loud, so that the mike could properly pick it up. Doing as he was instructed, George yelled 'OR-DER! OR-DER!' at the top of his voice – this was broadcast twice a week, as the intro to the show, for the next few years.

When George retired in 1983 (to go to the Lords as Lord Tonypandy), the seat went to the Tories, in the person of city councillor, hotelier and one-time Cardiff City football director **Stefan Terlezki,** who had settled in Cardiff after fleeing Ukraine as a boy during the Second World War. Terlezki made the national news when he managed to get his father out of Soviet Russia, where he had been imprisoned since the end of the war. He lost the seat in 1987, when Labour regained Cardiff West with **Rhodri Morgan.**

Rhodri was a proper Cardiffian and was a popular constituency figure. He stood up to the Cardiff Bay Development Corporation over flood dangers – bringing him into opposition with his neighbouring MP, Alun Michael. (This was the first of many splits in Cardiff's Labour group over the past thirty years.) Later, Blair passed him over for office, even though Rhodri had been a Shadow Minister for eight years. But the messy-haired Morgan (who hails from Radyr) got his own back by outmanoeuvring Blair's man, Alun Michael, to become leader of the Welsh Assembly – a job he held for nine years.

When Rhodri went over to the Assembly, he was succeeded at Westminster by his assistant **Kevin Brennan** – my old economics teacher from Radyr Comprehensive. The Cardiff

West seat, though, like Cardiff South, does not seem as safe for Labour as it once did, with a majority almost cut in half, to less than 5,000 votes, at the last election.

The third Labour seat, until 1950, was **Cardiff East**. But this seat disappeared due to boundary changes. After that, the third seat was **Cardiff North** (once called Cardiff North-West). This is the seat of the relatively affluent northern suburbs, mixed in with some more 'ordinary' areas. For years, it was regarded as 'safe Tory' – unless the Tories had a very bad year. It went to Labour in 1966, back to the Tories in 1970, and didn't fall to Labour again until 1997, when Tory Welsh Office minister **Gwilym Jones** (MP since 1983) lost the seat to **Julie Morgan**, Rhodri's wife and a councillor in her own right. Julie Morgan held the seat through three successful elections, before losing fairly narrowly to the Tories' **Jonathan Evans** (a Cardiff native) in 2010.

Finally, Cardiff acquired a fourth seat in 1974: **Cardiff Central**, a fairly mixed seat with an ever-increasing student population. This was held for eighteen years by the Tory **Ian Grist** – a remarkable act of survival, given that the seat was always so marginal. Grist was finally displaced in 1992, when Labour won the seat with ex-trade union official (and Cardiff councillor) **Jon Owen Jones**; he eventually lost the seat to the Lib Dems' **Jenny Willott** in 2005, when the student vote seemed to swing away from Labour.

Cardiff WAGs
No, this bit is not about footballers' wives. 'WAG' is the 'Welsh Assembly Government'.

Since 1999, we have had another august body representing us in Wales, namely the Welsh Assembly. The four constituencies in Cardiff are exactly the same as the Westminster ones, but we don't really have space to cover them here.

Council

For years, there was **Cardiff County Borough Council**. Cardiff was geographically within the county of Glamorgan, but provided all of its own council services.

Then, from 1974–95, there were two councils: **South Glamorgan County Council** (responsible for education, social services and major transport and planning matters) and **Cardiff City Council**.

The city was run by Tories for years; they became known as 'the City Fathers'. But Labour gradually took over most of the big British cities from the traditional ruling Tories after the Second World War; Cardiff's city council went to Labour in 1955, when **Leo Abse**, a radical city solicitor, masterminded the winning Labour campaign. He became MP for Pontypool in 1958 and was involved in a lot of reforming legislation during the 1960s.

From 1974–95, Labour often ruled both councils, but the councils (headquartered close to one another in Cardiff's Civic Centre) were frequently at loggerheads. For instance, the Cardiff Bay redevelopment – brainchild of Tory Welsh Secretary Nicholas Edwards in the mid-'80s – was enthusiastically promoted by the county, under the leadership first of (**Lord**) **Jack Brooks,** and then of Brooks' protegee **Russell Goodway**. But it was fairly resolutely opposed by Labour's city council crowd, led first by **John Phillips** and then by **Sue Essex**. It all hinged on differences of opinion over the Cardiff Barrage, and possible flood risks. Eventually the thing was driven through (and has since given us a big leisure area in Cardiff Bay, seemingly with a lessened risk of flooding); but the acrimony between the two Labour factions remained.

In 1995, South Glamorgan was scrapped, as were all the county councils, as Wales was left with twenty-two 'unitary authorities'. In other words, each area had just one council, instead of two. Cardiff City Council changed its name to **Cardiff County Council,** which it has been known as ever since. By this time, South Glamorgan had moved from Kingsway to a new county hall 'down the Bay', and this was where Cardiff County Council was now headquartered. (Although City Hall is still used for administrative purposes.)

From 1995–2004 the council was a Labour administration, headed by Russell Goodway – leader of the old county council. In 2004 the Liberal Democrats, led by **Rodney Berman,** took over from Labour and Berman was council leader for eight years (2004–12), presiding for some of that time in coalition with Plaid Cymru (led by **Neil McEvoy**). In 2012, Labour returned to power, with Berman dramatically losing his seat (after a number of recounts) in Cathays. Labour's new leader was **Heather Joyce,** dubbed 'Supergran' by the *Echo*. Curiously, this made her the third successive council leader in Cardiff who was not from Cardiff: Goodway (who has never lived in the city) being from Rhoose, Berman from Scotland and Mrs Joyce from the Rhymney Valley. Heather left office in 2014, to be replaced by **Phil Bale,** who is (finally!) a native Cardiffian.

LIFE ON THE EDGE

In many ways, the map of Cardiff is almost symmetrical, isn't it?

If you were to fold a map of the city in half along the length of the River Taff, the two halves of the city would form an almost exact match. Splott and Grangetown, Roath and Canton, Ely and Trowbridge, Rhiwbina and Radyr ... try it with the area you live in. It works almost every time.

As the city has grown from its inner core, new estates have sprung up on opposite outskirts of the capital. While some of these developments provided new green spaces for the former residents of the demolished streets of Adamsdown and Butetown, they also had an impact on their new environments where they sprang up.

This growth has put some historic, rural spots of the city under threat. Take the old, almost rustic area of St Mellons, for example. This community is on the very eastern edge of Cardiff – so far east that it was part of Monmouthshire until 1974. In those days, St Mellons was a hamlet amongst the green fields that separated Cardiff from Newport.

Perhaps the area's claim to fame was its four pubs situated in close proximity along Newport Road: the Bluebell, the Star, the Coach House (formerly the White Hart) and the Fox and Hounds (widely believed to be one of the oldest pubs in Cardiff). The area's charms were officially recognised via conservation area status in 1977.

But the growth of the city takes no prisoners. The 1980s saw the birth of an enormous new development on the nearby fields of 'Trowbridge Mawr', pushing right up alongside the boundary of this peaceful plot.

These days, when people refer to St Mellons, they are often not talking about the historic St Mellons, but the considerably larger and more modern housing estate that has been built to the south and east of it. Today 'St Mellons' even falls under two separate electoral wards. 'Old St Mellons' (as it has now officially become) combines with neighbouring Pontprennau, while new St Mellons forms part of Trowbridge ward.

St Mellons continues to grow, with proposals in place for over 1,000 new homes on land surrounding the village. Meanwhile, there are other plans for expansion throughout the city, and it is anticipated that there will be some 41,000 new homes in Cardiff by 2026.

FINAL SAY

Yes, these new housing developments are legitimate worries for many people. We are currently in a very odd place in Cardiff, in terms of how people feel. On the one hand, Cardiff has recently been voted as having the best quality of life of any major city in the UK. MoneySuperMarket – a comparison website – ranked the UK's twelve largest cities by measuring things like house-price growth and rental costs, salaries and disposable income growth, living costs, unemployment rates and 'life satisfaction', finding that Cardiff had the lowest average living costs at £359 a week, and the lowest unemployment rate, at 8.1 per cent.

At the same time, residents in various parts of the city are protesting about proposed new housing developments which, they feel, will make the city too large and too congested. So who is right?

Perhaps it depends upon who you are and where you live. Younger people living in central areas – students, young professionals in new developments in 'town' or 'the Bay' – may

feel that life in their part of Cardiff is full of charm and zest. For them, the city might indeed possess that much-mentioned quality of 'vibrancy'.

Older and more settled residents might be the ones looking upon the proposed new developments with more trepidation. Of course, they might be being overly pessimistic. One thing is sure: with the projected rate of population expansion in the Cardiff area over the next few years, the transport infrastructure will need to be radically improved if the city is not to become gridlocked at peak periods. Much depends, then, upon the delivery of the Cardiff Metro scheme, with its promised new stations and, in some cases, new lines.

It appears to me that we are at a watershed in the development of Cardiff. Things could be about to get a whole lot better – or they may be about to take a turn for the worse. It depends upon whether or not you buy into the council's vision of the future.

Whichever way it goes, I am sure the people of Cardiff will carry on with a laugh and a smile, as they ever did.

So now we have finished our ramble through the highways and byways of the history of Cardiff. We hope it was as enjoyable a journey for you as it was for us while writing it. We wrote enough material for two volumes, but there was still stuff left over to talk about.

I have managed to get rid of a couple of files of newspaper cuttings about Cardiff that had accumulated over the past few years. But there are still another couple of files to go, and there is more stuff about Cardiff appearing in the paper every day …

ACKNOWLEDGEMENTS & BIBLIOGRAPHY

Much of the information on what Cardiff used to be like came, initially, from conversations with my father Keith Bennett. From the age of about 12, I had to hear all this stuff, and I suppose at some point during my 20s, I started actually listening to it! There were also recollections from my mother, Joan Withers, and stepfather, Frank Withers.

When I began reading newspaper pieces on 'old Cardiff', I found that Bill Barrett, Brian Lee and Dan O'Neill were a big help, although Dan, of course, does not deal in 'nostalgia' alone. I met Bill at the office of the *Cardiff Post*, and after I mentioned 'nostalgia', a reporter named Martin Donovan quickly intervened (jokily) with 'Nostalgia?! You mean local history ...' Well yes, Martin, you were right, but at some point, one runs into the other – I note from reading David's Splott piece that Bill was an influence on him, too, because he was his junior school teacher. Small world.

Once I started writing this with David, I raided my father's book collection. I also had a book on Canton by Bryan Jones. This was very useful, not only on Canton itself (which ended up not being featured in this book, due to lack of space), but on the social changes which the country underwent during the twentieth century, and how they affected Cardiff.

Another useful source of information has been the Letters column of the *South Wales Echo*, where points of historical interest are sometimes raised. Personal experiences are a crucial source, although we have to bear in mind that often people disagree about what happened – so the more people who write in to verify such-and-such a point, the better. There is a chap who often writes to the *Echo* called Graham Williams. He gets 'bees in his bonnet' about place names, and half the stuff he writes I disagree with, but he is at least keeping discussions alive about places, place names and other things that might otherwise disappear entirely from our folk memory.

Bill Herbert's colourful life story *A Life Still Living* formed part of David's research on several chapters – an enjoyable read he assures me. David's memories of Splott are also, as you will have seen, deeply personal.

His recollections of pop music, nights out and other escapades have informed many chapters, but he wishes to thank Grange Albion stalwart Tony Hicks for his input into the baseball piece and the staff of The Hollybush in Pentwyn for supplying the excellent pints of Brains he was able to enjoy in his research about beer! Let's look at each chapter in a bit more depth though.

1: Cardiff – Where's 'At, Then?
This chapter has multiple sources, including John Davies, *A History of Wales* (Penguin, 1994); *The Chronology of Cardiff Castle* by the Theosophical Society; and Tim Lambert, 'A Short History of Cardiff' in *World History Encyclopedia*.

2: Food and Drink
This chapter is almost entirely the recollections and experiences of David Collins – who doesn't need reference books! However, he has spoken to others about some

parts – including staff at Cadwaladers and his mate who actually works for Clark's Pies. The Patrice Grill piece was simply what David could remember through the foggy haze of memory.

3: Civic Society

Information on the 'Birth of a City' section came from various sources. 'Going Back to My Routes' was written with reference to Bryan Jones' Canton book, *The Archive Photographs Series: Canton* (Chalford, Stroud, 1995); Stephen Rowson & Ian Wright, *The Glamorganshire & Aberdare Canals* (Black Dwarf, 2001); D.S.M. Barrie, *The Taff Vale Railway* (Oakwood Press, 1982). Alan Price-Talbot's recollections of travelling to London by train in the 1930s appeared in a letter to the *South Wales Echo*. The swastika story is recounted on the 'Babylon Wales' website. A tour of David's attic also unearthed the wonderful volume *Cardiff 1889–1974: The Story of the County Borough* (Corporation of Cardiff, 1974). We also found some great leaflets about the City Hall up there and, finally, David looked up a few former colleagues at City Hall for their recollections of days gone by.

4: Sporting Cardiff

Cardiff City FC: David Collins, *Born Under a Grange End Star* (Sigma Leisure, Wilmslow, 2002 – one he did earlier!); Grahame Lloyd, *C'mon City!: A Hundred Years of the Bluebirds* (Seren, Bridgend, 1999); Richard Shepherd, *The Definitive Cardiff City FC: A Statistical History* (Tony Brown, Nottingham, 2002).

I have also derived much information, over the years, from the John Crooks books, self-published by the author in the late 1980s and early '90s – a time when not too many people were interested in Cardiff City. I also interviewed

Jim Wilson, son of CCFC founder Bartley, for *O Bluebird of Happiness* fanzine in 1990; still an important source of info about City's early years.

Cardiff Rugby FC: David Parry-Jones (ed.), *Taff's Acre: A History and Celebration of Cardiff Arms Park* (Collins, 1984); D.E. Davies, *Cardiff RFC: History & Statistics 1876–1975* (Starling Press, Risca, 1975); Dai Smith and Gareth Williams, *Fields of Praise: The Official History of the Welsh Rugby Union* (University of Wales Press, 1980); David Parry-Jones, *The Rugby Clubs of Wales* (London: Hutchinson, 1989)

5: Around the Districts
Ely: Nigel Billingham and Stephen K. Jones, *The Archive Photographs Series: Ely, Caerau and Michaelston-super-Ely* (Stroud: Chalford, 1996); recollections by Keith Bennett.

Rhiwbina: Additional information from the late Malcolm Bennett (G.B.'s uncle), a long-time Rhiwbina resident. David also visited the Garden Village one sunny afternoon to gain a better feel of the place.

6: Going Out
We're Going Down the Pub: David Matthews, *The Complete Guide to Cardiff's Pubs* (Welsh Brewers, 1995); Brian Glover *Cardiff Pubs and Breweries* (Tempus, 2005); Brian Glover, *Brains: 125 Years* (Breedon, 2007).

Picture Palaces: Sources include Gary Wharton, *Ribbon of Dreams: Remembering Cardiff Cinemas* (Mercia Cinema Society, 1998); Mr Barker, various letters to the *South Wales Echo*; and recollections by Joan Withers and Keith Bennett.

Cardiff's Nightspots: Information from Joan Withers and Keith Bennett; personal recollections of D.C. and G.B.; bits of info from other books, like Bryan Jones' Canton book.

And the Band Played On: Recollections of Sarah Boubaker and a handy list of Capitol gigs from days gone by.

7: Where's 'At Again?
David is grateful for information on the growth of Welsh in the city provided by the magazines of RhAG – Rhieni Dros Addysg Gymraeg. David also consulted the Cardiff Local Development Plan 2006–2026, which will set the planning framework for the city up until 2026, in researching this chapter.

Anyone who should have been mentioned but wasn't – sorry, I forgot!

Also from the authors

Also from The History Press

ANCIENT LEGENDS RETOLD

This series features some of the country's best-known folklore heroes. Each story is retold by master storytellers, who live and breathe these legends. From the forests of Sherwood to the Round Table, this series celebrates our rich heritage.

Find these titles and more at
www.thehistorypress.co.uk

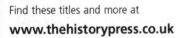

Also from The History Press

WALES

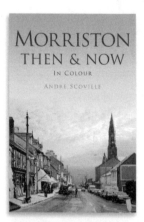

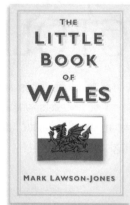

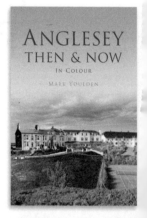

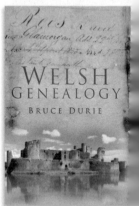

8|15